The Lost
COWBOY
GHOST

For more thrills and chills
check out these Apple Paperbacks series:

The House on Cherry Street
by Rod Philbrick and Lynn Harnett

Phantom Rider
by Janni Lee Simmer

Animorphs
by K. A. Applegate

Goosebumps
by R. L. Stine

The Lost
COWBOY
GHOST

by James Buckley, Jr.

SCHOLASTIC INC.
New York Toronto London Auckland Sydney

Cover art by Jim Auckland

ISBN 0-590-16211-X

12 11 10 9 8 7 6 5 4 3 2 1   6 7 8 9/9 0 1/0

Printed in the U.S.A.   40

First Scholastic printing, December 1996

1

There was nothing out there.

Gordo, Rusty, and Jenna stared out the window. They'd been riding since early that morning on the back bench seat of the bus. They had bounced up and down over and over on the rough road. Their insides were beginning to feel like jelly. As if that wasn't bad enough, all they had seen for the last two hours was nothing.

No buildings. No people. No mini-malls. They were beginning to wonder if a week at Shorty's Six Points Ranch was worth having to look at all this nothing.

"Man, this is boring," Gordo said for the fourteenth time that hour.

"Yeah," Rusty said. "I haven't been this bored since Mr. Davidson tried to teach us long division."

"I think it's kind of pretty," Jenna said. Gordo and Rusty threw wadded-up paper napkins at her head.

"If I see any more desert dust, I'm gonna puke!" Rusty said. He ducked as Jenna threw the napkin back at his head.

"This was your idea, Rusty," she said. Jenna imitated his squeaky voice. " 'Dudes, it will be so cool. We'll ride horses. And rope cattle. And wear cowboy hats.' " She paused to let Gordo stop laughing at her imitation of their friend. "So where are the hats and horses, *dude*?"

"I didn't know we'd have to drive to the moon to get there," Rusty said. "Leave me alone!"

This was the fourth summer trip the friends had taken together. Last summer, the three schoolmates had gone to a dude ranch. It was fun, but sort of phony. So Rusty had found this real, working ranch. But it was turning out to be farther from Dallas than they had thought.

They stared out the window again. The yellow and brown sand stretched out forever. The hills rose up like camels' humps on the horizon. Once in a while there was a clump of cactus plants. Or a pile of rocks. Or a dry creek bed.

But other than that, just miles and miles of nothing. The other kids on the bus were reading books or talking or playing their GameBoys. The bus driver stared out the front window. The black road rolled off into the distance ahead of them.

Eldrick Gordon, better known as Gordo, was looking out his window when he thought he saw something familiar in the middle of nothing. The ten-year-old's white T-shirt was bright against his dark skin. If you looked in his eyes, you'd know he was the smartest one of their group. Gordo just knew stuff.

He pointed out what he saw to Jenna. "Is that what I think it is?" he asked. Jenna looked out the window to where Gordo was pointing. Off in the distance was a giant cactus, the biggest one they'd seen yet.

The cactus had a tall, round stalk as its bottom. Across the top of that stalk was another long, thin stalk. It formed a giant letter T with the base. At the ends of the T, two more cactus branches rose straight up to the sky.

"It's a goalpost!" Jenna said. "A football goalpost!"

Rusty heard Jenna yelling. He climbed over her to get a look. "Cool! Just like in Texas Stadium!" he said.

"I wonder if you could kick a field goal wearing cowboy boots," Gordo said. He held up his own foot to show off his new pointy-toed boots.

"Your boots are so pointy," Rusty said, "you'd probably pop the ball."

"At least I'm wearing real cowboy boots," Gordo said. "You'll be the only cowboy in the world wearing sneakers!"

While Gordo and Rusty argued, Jenna was still looking at the goalpost cactus. "I hope we have time to play some football at camp," she said with a sigh.

Eleven-year-old Jenna Ramirez tossed her long black hair back over her shoulder. Her hair was down now. But she pulled it into a ponytail when she played. Then all anyone saw of it was a black blur when she ran. Jenna was one of the best athletes in their school. Jenna loved horses, that was for sure. But she loved football almost as much.

"Did you bring your ball?" Rusty asked.

"Duh — of course," Jenna said. "I don't go anywhere without it. It's in my backpack." She pointed up to the rack over their heads.

"Do you think the Cowboys will win the Super Bowl again this year?" Gordo asked.

"I sure hope so," Jenna said. "They've been my favorite team since I was a kid."

"You're still a kid now," Rusty said, laughing.

"You know what I mean," Jenna said, and punched him in the arm.

"Is Emmitt Smith still your favorite player?" asked Gordo.

"So many questions, Gord. You should be a newspaper reporter," Jenna said. "You know he is."

"Yeah, but Troy Aikman rules!" Rusty said. "He's the best there is."

Suddenly Rusty pointed out his window. "Look," he said. "There's a sign!"

The kids all crowded around Rusty to look out his window. They saw a wooden sign in the shape of a cowboy boot:

SHORTY'S SIX POINTS RANCH
10 Miles

"Yeee-hah!" Gordo did his best cowboy yell. "Only ten more miles on this stupid bus!"

Rusty and Jenna did a high five. "Six Points Ranch, here we come!" they said.

Rusty Daniels was totally psyched. Jenna and Gordo were right; this had been his idea. Ever since he saw the commercial for the ranch while he was watching the Cowboys win Super Bowl XXX in January, he knew this was the place for a real Wild West adventure. Rusty was the kind of guy who could talk you into anything. And he'd talked Gordo and Jenna into coming with him. Rusty, who would turn eleven in a month, was usually pretty funny, but sometimes his jokes were just dumb. Still, he was a great friend to have.

Over the last ten bumpy miles, the three friends put away all the things they'd used to pass the time. Gordo's book on the history of Texas went back in his overstuffed bookbag. Jenna finished reading *Sports Illustrated for Kids*. And Rusty played one more quarter of football on his hand-held video game.

The bus rolled on and all the nothing slowly

became something. Fences began to appear alongside the road. A few cattle were grazing in some fields. They began to see patches of green and brown grass. Finally, when they thought they couldn't ride another second, another sign appeared. The entire bus cheered when they saw the sign:

Shorty's Six Points Ranch

As the bus rolled into camp, they saw a smaller sign on a post near the entrance

Home of the Famous Lost Cowboy Ghost!

"Lost Cowboy Ghost!" the three friends said at once.

"There was nothing about that in the video they sent us," Gordo said. "I think I would have remembered."

"I wonder how he got lost," Jenna said.

"I don't care," Rusty said. "Ghost or no ghost, I'm just glad we're finally here. I can't wait to get off this bus!" They passed several buildings and a corral filled with cattle. There was another area where horses stood waiting at a post.

Finally, the bus slowed down and stopped. The doors opened. A dozen happy kids jumped off.

Gordo, Rusty, and Jenna were the last to get off. As they climbed down through the door, they saw the other kids standing in a circle, open-mouthed in surprise.

"What is it?" Gordo said. "Is it the ghost?"

The three friends spun around to see what everyone was looking at.

There stood Troy Aikman!

2

"Troy Aikman!" shouted the kids. Gordo, Rusty, Jenna, and all the kids from the bus crowded around the football star. "What are you doing here?" they asked.

"Well, the man who runs this camp used to be one of my coaches with the Dallas Cowboys," Troy said. "He retired a few years ago to start up this camp. Since I still have some vacation left before training camp, he asked if I could come up and help out this week. Three of his cowboys have quit lately."

"Why did they quit?" asked Gordo.

"They were scared," said a short man who came out from behind the bus. He had a scraggly brown beard. A red handkerchief was tied around his neck. And over his left eye was a black patch like a pirate would wear. "They were just yellow!" He spit into the dust and stared at the kids with his one beady eye. "And no man who rides with me is a chicken!"

"Why were they scared?" asked Gordo. *Geez, Gordo, always asking questions*, thought Jenna.

"Aw, they got spooked by an old story. Them fellers said they thought the Lost Cowboy Ghost was gonna get them," said the short man. He spit again. *I'm going to watch where I walk*, thought Jenna.

"Is there really a ghost?" asked one blond boy.

"Well," the man said, "I can't say there is. And I can't say there isn't. All's I know is that unless we get some new cowboys to come work here, this camp is gonna close down! But I'm not gonna let that happen," he added. "Not while I'm alive."

The kids looked worried. Who was this weird guy? And what was the deal with the eye patch?

Troy didn't look worried, though. He just laughed. "I don't know about any ghost. But I do know the Six Points Ranch is open for business right now! Everyone, I'd like you to meet Shorty Weems, the head honcho here," Troy said. "And don't worry, he's not as tough as he looks."

Shorty gave the campers a big grin. Then, in a loud voice, he said "Howdy, y'all! And welcome to Six Points Ranch! C'mon, let me show you around."

After Troy had shaken everyone's hand, and promised them all autographs later on, the tour of Shorty's Six Points Ranch began.

"Okay, all you cowboys and cowgirls, here we

are," Shorty said. He pointed to a pair of buildings near the main road. "Over yonder are your bunkhouses. You can stow your gear there after dinner. That big tent behind you is the cook tent. When we're not out on the trail, that's where Cookie will serve you grub."

Rusty whispered to Gordo. "A guy whose name is Cookie? What's his last name? Crumbs?" They busted out laughing.

Then Gordo whispered back. "Maybe his first name is Chocolate Chip!" They laughed again. But they stopped an instant later when Shorty gave them a nasty look with his one eye.

"Somethin' funny, fellas?" he asked. He moved toward them, a menacing look on his face.

"Um, uh, no, sir, Mr. Shorty, sir," Rusty said. His face turned as red as his hair. Gordo tried to hide behind Jenna.

But then Shorty smiled again. "Oh, that's too bad. I love a good joke!"

He turned and walked toward the corral. "This guy is weird," whispered Rusty as they followed the group.

The campers gathered along the rail fence around the corral. "You probably know that these here animals are cows," said Shorty. He sat on the top rail of the fence while he talked. "Anyone know what kind?"

"Big and smelly?" Rusty cracked. Everyone laughed.

"I said I love a *good* joke, pal, not a stupid one," said Shorty.

"They're Herefords," Gordo said. That Gordo just knew lots of stuff.

"That's right, pardner," said Shorty with a smile at Gordo. "And you'll be spending a lot of time around them for the next few days, so here are some things to remember. Don't walk behind a cow. That might spook them. And watch out for their horns. They're mighty sharp. I should know," he said. He pointed to his eye patch.

"Gross!" said some of the kids.

"Cool!" said the others.

Shorty ignored them and kept talking. "And never go in a corral alone. These cows are ten times bigger than you are and faster to boot. Okay, let's move on to the classroom."

At the mention of the word classroom, all the kids groaned. "Not more schoolwork," Rusty sighed. "I thought I was done with that until the fall."

"I didn't know cowboys went to school," Gordo said.

The wind was picking up. They moved as a group toward the far side of the camp's central square. The flag at the top of the flagpole fluttered in the breeze. Suddenly, Jenna's new cowboy hat blew off her head and spun along the ground behind her. "Hey," she said. "Come back here!"

11

The hat slid along the ground and under the corral fence. A couple of cows nearest the hat looked up. Their big, wet eyes watched Jenna run toward the corral after the hat. Another pair of eyes looked up at her. A tiny kitten was lapping water from a puddle in the corral.

"Dang it," she said. "That hat cost me twenty dollars." She looked around her. The group was now far away near the classroom buildings. The hat was just out of her reach inside the corral. *I can be in and out in a second,* she thought. *What could happen?*

She looked at the cows who were looking at her. "Nice cows," she said softly. "Good cows." *Man,* she thought, *Rusty was right. They* do *stink.*

Finally, she decided to go for it. She slipped between the rails of the fence and dashed toward the hat. Suddenly, she heard a loud *crack* from behind the cows. The sudden noise scared the cattle, and they began running away from it.

Right at Jenna!

The ground shook with their hoofbeats. Their sharp horns pointed right at her. A thunderous noise hit Jenna's ears.

Jenna froze.

STAMPEDE!

3

Quickly, Jenna started running back to the fence. Then she saw that the kitten was frozen stiff.

Jenna thought quickly. *If I hurry,* she thought, *I can grab the kitten and make it back in time.* She sprinted back toward the meowing kitty.

Shorty and Troy heard the noise behind them and came running back toward the corral. But they'd never make it. Jenna and the cat were going to be trampled.

Suddenly, a figure leaped over the fence and ran past Jenna. He wasn't wearing cowboy boots, he was wearing cool sneakers. The figure scooped up the kitten under his arm and kept running. Jenna watched in amazement as he didn't turn around and run away from the cows. He ran right toward them!

Two dozen frightened, charging cows were racing headlong toward one man with a cat under his arm. And instead of running away, the man was taking them head-on!

Now Troy and Shorty were even more scared. They just ran faster toward the corral. What was this guy doing? He would be squashed!

"Run away!" screamed Troy and Shorty as they ran toward the corral. "This way! This way! Jump the fence!"

But the man ignored them. On and on he ran, with the cat tucked under his arm like a football. Meanwhile, Jenna reached the fence and turned to watch the awful show.

The charging cows came closer and closer. They were just a few feet apart now. The man could see the cows' angry eyes as they stared at him.

Then, just as the first cow was about to smash into them, the mystery man suddenly zipped to his left and the cow missed. Another cow came charging in, and the man did it again. He zigged and he zagged, and cow after cow missed him and the cat. First he went left, then right, then right, then left. He dodged back and forth through the cows like a running back sprinting through a crowd of angry linebackers.

Finally, one cow remained ahead of them. It was the biggest, nastiest one of all, the fiercest and toughest linebacker in the bunch. The man and the cow were on a collision course. The dust was everywhere. The frightened crowd of kids

14

watched as the snorting beast and the speeding man came closer and closer. Would the last cow get them after all the man's amazing moves?

Jenna saw the cat hanging on for dear life. It grabbed the man's shirt with its claws. If the man tripped and fell, they were done for.

As Jenna watched, she saw the final cow ahead of the man. *Whew!* she thought. *There is plenty of room to run around it.*

But the mysterious running man didn't run around the last cow . . . he headed straight for it!

He didn't zig, he didn't zag, he didn't go anywhere but straight ahead. Then, at the last possible second, he leaped! Jenna shut her eyes tight. *I don't want to watch*, she thought.

The man put one sneaker on the cow's nose and stepped with the other on the cow's back. He ran *over* the cow!

He was through! He'd made it through the stampede! The kitten was saved! The campers cheered. Shorty and Troy and a pair of cowboys rounded up the cattle into another corral.

Jenna couldn't believe what had just happened. One minute she was nose to nose with a bunch of nasty cows, trying to save a frightened cat, the next someone had beaten her to it! What had happened? Who was this guy? It had all happened so fast, she wasn't even sure he was real. Was he the ghost?

The man put the cat down and wiped his forehead.

"Are you okay?" he asked.

Jenna looked up. What she saw shocked her so much she almost fainted.

"You're . . . you're . . ." she stammered.

"Yeah," he said. "It's me." He held up the little black cat.

"I'm just lucky I didn't spike this little guy when we made it to the end zone."

4

Jenna finally untied her tongue. "Emmitt Smith!" she screamed.

"In person," Emmitt said. He shook Jenna's hand and then waved to the kids. They had gathered along the rail fence and were cheering like mad. Troy and Emmitt together! No one at the camp could believe their luck. This was the coolest thing that had ever happened to them!

Troy climbed over the fence and walked over to Emmitt. "Hey, Emmitt!" he said. "I thought I recognized your moves. Glad you could make it." Then he looked at Jenna. "Lucky for you Emmitt showed up when he did. Didn't you listen to what Shorty said about staying out of the corral?"

Jenna nodded. "I was just getting my hat. I'm sorry."

"No problem, Jenna," Emmitt said. "It was just like running against the Pittsburgh Steelers in Super Bowl Thirty. Only these cows were better-looking!" He and Troy joined the kids in laughing. Rusty imagined a cow dressed up in a black-and-gold Steelers uniform. The horns would stick out of the helmet!

Jenna went over to get what was left of her hat. The cows' hooves had smashed it as flat as a pancake! She gulped when she thought of what they might have done to Emmitt.

She joined Emmitt and Troy as they walked back to the group.

"Thanks for coming, Emmitt," Troy said. "We're down to four cowboys this week."

"Are they all really afraid of a ghost?" Emmitt asked.

"They're afraid of something," Troy said. "These cowboys are as tough as our defensive line. It takes a lot to scare them."

"You're not scared of a ghost, are you, Emmitt?" Jenna asked.

"Nothing wrong with being scared once in a while," Emmitt said. "But the only thing I'm scared of right now is not making it to another Super Bowl!"

Emmitt turned back to Troy.

"Shorty's been talking about this camp for years, but I've never heard him mention this ghost before. Where did he come from?" Emmitt asked.

"Well, it's an old story in these parts. But Shorty started telling folks about it this summer in hopes of getting some publicity," Troy said.

"Now it turns out there might really be one. Ever since he started telling the story, a lot of weird things have been happening around here."

"Well, the *real* Cowboys are here now," Emmitt said. "If we can't tackle this ghost, no one can! Right, Jenna?" Emmitt turned around and looked at Jenna. She still was stunned at seeing her hero up close.

"Right, Jenna?" Emmitt asked again. He waved a hand in front of her face to get her attention.

"Oh, um, yea, right, Emmitt," she said. *I'm talking to Emmitt Smith,* she thought to herself. *I'm glad Rusty and Gordo are here to see this. Otherwise, they'd never believe me!*

The campers watched while Emmitt said hi to Shorty. "It's been a while, Shorty," Emmitt said. "How are you doing? You're not going to make me run sprints, are you?"

Shorty laughed. "Emmitt, I never had any trouble getting you to do your workouts. But it's nice to see that you're still doing everything I taught you!"

Emmitt turned to the kids. "Shorty was one of the best coaches I ever had," he said. "And there's nothing better than a good coach!"

"How about we continue the tour?" Shorty said. "I'm bettin' none of you will wander into any corrals now, will ya?"

"Say, Shorty," Troy said. "Why do you think

those cows got spooked like that? Jenna didn't do anything to them."

Shorty rubbed his scruffy beard. "Well, now, Troy," he began. "I can't rightly say what spooked them critters." He looked around at the group with his one good eye. "But it just might have been the Lost Cowboy Ghost!"

Rusty and Gordo looked at each other. "Is this guy for real?" Gordo said.

"You mean, there really *is* a ghost?" Rusty asked.

"There's no ghost out here," Jenna said firmly.

"That's what Tinker Garrity said, Jenna," Shorty replied. "Before he woke up one morning to find the Lost Cowboy Ghost hovering over his bed! Tinker was on his horse and gone faster than Emmitt here can score a twenty-yard touchdown. And Beans Peterson was scared out of his wits when he saw the Lost Cowboy Ghost ride *through* the side of the cook tent. They were some tough cowpokes. And *they* thought the Lost Cowboy Ghost was so real, they quit!

"The clincher came last week," Shorty continued. "Nate Robinson was looking for a cow that had wandered off. He said he got pushed from behind and tumbled down the side of a gulley. He broke his wrist and twisted an ankle real bad, not to mention the scrapes. When he looked back up at the top of the gulley, he said he saw a cowboy who was glowing white from head to toe, standing up there shaking his fist at him. Once Nate got patched up, he was gone. With Tinker and Beans, that was three cowboys we lost 'cause of this ghost."

Jenna, Gordo, and Rusty looked at each other. This might not be such a fun trip after all.

"If he is real, where did he come from?" Gordo asked Shorty.

"Well, let me tell you all a story," Shorty said. The campers and the NFL stars sat down on the ground and on benches and on the corral railing. Shorty told this tale:

"Way back in 1875, this whole valley was filled with cattle. There were cows as far as the eye could see."

"Or the nose could smell," Rusty whispered.

"Thousands of cowboys worked the ranges," Shorty continued. "They herded the cattle to market and made sure the cows were safe from coyotes and bandits and such. The cowboys worked day and night watching over the herd. They got to know each cow by name . . . and that was a lot of cows' names to remember.

"One cowboy named Tex — there were a lot of cowboys named Tex — had a favorite calf named Violet. He watched over her like she was his pet. Violet followed Tex everywhere. He even taught her tricks. Violet was the only cow in the herd who could fetch a stick."

"Oh, please," Jenna groaned. "As if."

"Well it's a lot easier than teaching a dog to give milk," Shorty said. "Anyway, one day, Tex woke up and couldn't find Violet anywhere. She was just gone. He was very sad about this and vowed to find her no matter how long it took. He left camp that day and started out on his search for his lost calf. Well, pardners, let me tell you. No one ever saw old Tex again. And no one ever saw Violet. And the legend says that they've been wandering these hills ever since, a-lookin' for each other. Tex is the Lost Cowboy Ghost!"

5

"**M**an, that's some story, Shorty," Emmitt said. "I almost believe it myself. Have you ever seen the ghost?"

"No, sir," Shorty said. "Not even when I had two good eyes. But I've been hearing stories since I was smaller than these young cowpokes."

"Well, Shorty," Troy said. "I don't believe in ghosts. I believe in football! And I believe I'd like to show these campers the rest of your ranch."

Everyone stood up and dusted off. They followed Shorty and Troy to the far end of the camp. The group reached a long, wooden building with a steep roof. "This here is the classroom," Shorty said. "Here's where we'll start learning how to be cowboys." Rusty was not thrilled to finally see the classroom. He imagined spending a week stuck in a desk, listening to Shorty talk about boring stuff. If they made him do homework, he was catching the next bus out.

Shorty swung open the big double doors of the classroom building. Inside was the coolest classroom Rusty, Gordo, and Jenna had ever seen. There were no chairs, no desks, and no blackboard. The floor was covered with sawdust and the ceiling was twenty feet over their heads.

Out in the middle of the floor was a big brown creature that looked like a cow. But as they got closer, they saw that it was just a dummy. It had wooden legs and horns, and brown cloth took the place of its hide. Someone had even painted an eye patch on its face to make it look like Shorty.

Shorty turned and faced the group after they filed into the classroom. "Every cowboy has to learn some important things before he can ride the range," Shorty said. "And here is where you'll practice those things."

"What will we learn about?" Gordo asked.

"I'll show you," Troy said. He took a coil of rope from a hook on the wall. Holding most of the rope in his left hand, he slipped a loop of it into his right. Suddenly he began twirling the loop over his head, faster and faster. Then — zip — he threw the loop like a perfect bullet pass over the middle.

The loop zinged through the air and fell over the cow's neck.

"Touchdown!" Emmitt yelled.

"Way to go!" Shorty said. "That's what a cow-

24

boy needs to know how to do. How to rope a cow to bring it back into the herd."

Wow, Rusty thought, *this classroom might not be so bad after all.*

"There's other things a cowboy needs to practice, too," Troy said. "Like how to make a bedroll, how to saddle a horse, how to keep the herd together. But the most important thing a cowboy needs to learn is teamwork. Just like Emmitt and I do with our Dallas teammates."

"That's right, you guys," Emmitt said. "The only way you can do anything — on the range or on the football field — is if you work together."

"You sure worked together well at the Super Bowl!" Jenna yelled.

"Yeah," Emmitt said, "that was fun. No matter how many Super Bowls we win, they're always special. And that's because we have teammates to share them with."

"I expect you'll all share a championship together one day," Troy said. "Whether it's a Super Bowl or something else."

Shorty stood up. "Well, cowboys, I hate to break up this little powwow about the NFL, but I'd like to share something else with you — food!"

Rusty, Gordo, and Jenna raced to the front of the group. In all the excitement of meeting the Cowboys — and watching Emmitt take on the charging herd — they'd forgotten how hungry they were.

"What do you think they'll have?" Gordo asked. "Pizza?"

"Pizza at a cowboy camp? — no way," Rusty said. "I think they'll have beans and rice and watermelon."

"I'd rather just have a big salad," Jenna said. "I've seen enough beef for today."

Rusty, Jenna, and Gordo were the first campers to walk into the big cook tent. It was made of canvas draped over stakes in the ground. Long picnic tables filled one side of the room. There were benches to sit on. On the other side of the room was a long serving table. Plates and napkins and silverware were all lined up and ready to go. But there was no food.

Shorty, Troy, and Emmitt went behind the serving table. "Where's chow, Cookie?" Shorty shouted toward the kitchen area at the back of the cook tent. The three men walked all around the tent, shouting for Cookie. But he didn't answer.

Finally, Shorty came out of the kitchen carrying a huge silver pot. Thank goodness, sighed the kids. Food.

"I can't find Cookie anywhere," Shorty said. "There's just this big pot of stew waiting to be served up."

"Did he quit, too?" Emmitt asked.

"No, he's not afraid of any ghost," Shorty said. "He's been serving up beans and rice here for thirty years. But it sure is mysterious, him disappearing like this."

"I don't like it," Troy said.

Just then, the sides of the tent flaps began whipping up in a sudden wind. Over the noise of the tent, a high-pitched ghostly wailing sound echoed through the entire camp. Everyone in the cook tent froze. Had they found the Lost Cowboy Ghost?

Or had it found them?

6

The wailing continued, the sound bouncing back and forth inside the tent. It got so loud that Rusty put down his bowl and covered his ears. The kids looked all around trying to find out where the sound was coming from. Was the ghost coming to get them?

Then Troy and Shorty laughed. Rusty stared at them in surprise.

"What's so funny?" he shouted over the noise.

"Well, I told that ghost story at just the right time," Shorty said. "No sooner do I bring him up than the Lost Cowboy Ghost sings his song!"

Now the campers were really worried. This guy Shorty was really nuts. First he says there's no ghost, then he says there is, and now he says it sings!

"Shorty, stop teasing these guys," Troy said. He looked at the campers. "Y'all, that's no ghost. Whenever we get a wind from the east like that, it whistles through the caverns in the hills just outside camp. There are all sorts of caves and passageways out there for the wind to whip through. You'll get used to it."

Shorty laughed as Troy finished talking. "Gotcha!" he yelled. "The Singing Lost Cowboy Ghost. Ha-ha. Maybe we can put on a concert. Ho, ho."

Rusty wanted to throw a bowl of stew at Shorty. But he couldn't because no one had been served yet.

The next mysterious sound we hear, Jenna thought, *will be about a dozen stomachs rumbling.*

Then a couple of dusty guys walked in wearing cowboy hats, chaps, boots, and spurs. One was very tall and thin. He was tanned brown and he looked like the next stiff wind would blow him over. The other was shorter but looked much stronger. His dark eyebrows shaded his eyes. A black hat made him look even tougher. He wore heavy leather gloves and had a gruff expression.

The man in the black hat cut in at the front of the chow line and scooped up a bowl of stew.

"Out of my way," he said. "I gotta eat!" Then he looked at them and let out a low growl. He grabbed a spoon and went to the table farthest away from the front and sat down. Everyone just stared at him.

"Don't mind Rex," the stringbean cowboy said. "He's always like that. That cowboy is meaner than a scorpion with a headache!"

"Hey, Fats," Shorty said. "How ya doin'?"

"Just fine, Shorty, just fine," answered the other man.

"Guys, I'd like you to meet Fats Vasquez, the skinniest cowboy in the West," Shorty said.

Fats took off his hat and made a deep bow. He looked like a drinking straw bending in half. "At your service," he said with a drawl. He looked at Troy and Emmitt. "Hey, Troy! You're back, huh? Good to see you. Folks, Troy here is almost as good a rider as he is a passer!" Then Fats saw Emmitt. "Weee-oohh! We got us another Cowboy with a capital C! Howdy, Emmitt!" He stuck out a bony hand.

"Nice to meet you, Fats," Emmitt said. "Say, shouldn't you be 'Slim'?"

"Well, I'll tell ya, young fella," Fats said. "The first outfit I ever worked for already had a Slim in it. Just like you don't have two Dallas Cowboys with the same number, you can't have two Texas cowboys in the same camp with the same nickname!"

Gordo looked Fats up and down. "Fats," he said, shaking his head. "Right."

Jenna introduced herself and asked, "How come you haven't left the camp, Fats? Aren't you scared of the ghost?"

"Shucks, little lady," Fats said. "There ain't no ghost. We're just havin' a run of bad luck, that's all. Now where's Cookie? I wanna eat."

"You look like you never eat!" said Rusty, laughing.

"Tell you what, *amigo*," Fats said. "You and me can have an eatin' contest right here. Whoever eats the most wins! Loser has to sing the group a song."

"You're on!" Rusty yelled.

But first they had to get their bowls and serve up the stew. While they began to line up at the big pot, Shorty was still looking for Cookie. "I'm really worried," he said to Troy. "He's the last guy I thought would quit."

Just then, Rusty looked up at the roof of the tent.

"Hey, Fats!" he shouted. "If there's no ghost, what's that?" He pointed up. Everyone looked up to where Rusty was pointing. When the kids saw what was up there, several bowls fell to the hard floor with a crash.

As the wind continued outside and the eerie song could still be heard, a dark shape appeared on the roof of the tent. The shadowy figure of a man was outlined against the canvas. He was floating there right above their heads!

"It's the Lost Cowboy Ghost!" shouted Rusty. "He's found us!"

7

As they stared at the roof in horror, the shape began to get closer and closer. The canvas stretched and the shape got bigger. The ghost was coming down to get them!

Suddenly, there was a loud ripping sound RIIIPPPP! then, CRASH! A man wearing a long white apron fell through the roof of the tent and landed butt-first in the giant pot of stew. The stew splashed everywhere, all over the campers, all over Troy, Emmitt, and Shorty. Fats was so skinny none of it even got near him.

Everyone yelled and screamed and began picking potatoes and carrots out of their hair. Rusty had a terrible thought: Now what would they have to eat?

"I guess that's Cookie," Jenna said as she scraped a gravy-covered carrot off her cheek. "Nice ghost, Rusty."

"Cookie!" Shorty yelled. "What in tarnation do

you think you're doing? You danged near broke your neck!"

"I was just saving this here kitty cat," Cookie said from his seat in the stew pot. He was stuck fast.

Cookie held up a little ball of fur that also was covered in gravy. The kitten that Emmitt had saved earlier was now mewing loudly and trying to lick the gravy off itself at the same time. It was no ghost, it was just a cat-loving cook.

"That kitten is a troublemaker," said Emmitt.

Cookie said he had climbed onto the roof when he heard the cat crying. Then he'd gotten stuck himself. He was just about to call for help when the roof of the tent ripped . . . and he made his debut in the pot-of-stew high dive.

Once she saw Cookie was okay, Jenna pointed out the obvious. She held up her empty bowl. "And now what'll we do about dinner? So far the cat is the only one here who's gotten anything to eat."

"Don't forget Rex," Jenna said quietly and pointed into the corner. But Rex had disappeared!

"Hey!" said Gordo. "Where did Rex go?" He and Rusty looked all around the tent but couldn't see the cowboy anywhere. "Did you see him leave?" Gordo asked.

"I was ducking falling cooks!" Rusty said.

The stew pot clanked on the table as Cookie wriggled, trying to get out. As he struggled, he answered Jenna's question about what they would eat.

"What are we going to eat?" he said. "The cowboy cook's best friend — pizza!"

"See, I told you," Gordo said to Rusty. "Cowboys *do* eat pizza."

With Emmitt and Fats pulling and prodding him, Cookie suddenly popped out of the pot like a cork from a bottle. Wiping the gravy from his hands — and from the cat — he went back into the kitchen to heat up the frozen pizzas. Meanwhile, everyone got a glass of soda and took a seat to await the feast.

The campers crowded to get a seat near Troy and Emmitt.

"Emmitt," Gordo said, "can I see your Super Bowl ring?"

Emmitt held out his left hand and all the campers piled on top of one another to check out the big, shiny chunk of metal. The ring was so huge, it looked like Emmitt had a golf ball on his hand.

"Man, that's something," Rusty said. "I'm going to get myself one of those some day."

"Yeah, but you'll never have three like Emmitt and Troy," teased Jenna.

"I will, too, you bonehead," Rusty yelled.

"I don't think I can ever get one of those," Gordo sighed.

"Why not?" Emmitt asked.

"I'm no good at football," Gordo answered. "I almost quit the school flag football team last spring because we lost so many games. And a lot of them were my fault."

"Losing a football game is never one person's fault, Gordo," Troy said. "Although I know how you feel. Who remembers what our record was in my first season in Dallas?"

"You stunk," Rusty laughed. "You were like zero and fifty!"

"Thanks, Rusty," Troy said with a grimace. "But it wasn't that bad. We only won one game my whole rookie season. We were one and fifteen. And I was the quarterback. The team was expecting me to win more than that.

"It got so bad, I almost thought of quitting!"

Troy Aikman, a quitter! No way!

The ghost was forgotten as everyone sadly thought of the Cowboys without Troy.

8

"Yes, but you didn't quit, did you, Troy?" Emmitt said. "You hung in there and got better and better."

"That's right, Emmitt," Troy said. "I didn't quit. My parents always told me never to give up."

"Thanks to you," Emmitt said, "your second season we won seven games. Then, in your third season, we went all the way to the Super Bowl!"

"Thanks to all of us," Troy said.

"And you beat Buffalo fifty-two to seventeen and Troy threw for two hundred seventy-three yards and four touchdowns!" Rusty shouted.

"And Emmitt ran for one hundred eight yards and scored a touchdown," Jenna added.

"Yes, that was a fun game," Troy remembered. "But because it was so hard to achieve that success, it made the win even more special!"

Gordo nodded. "Maybe I won't quit, after all," he said.

"Hey, Emmitt," Rusty said. "Tell us what your favorite touchdown is."

"My favorite touchdown is any touchdown that helps my team win," Emmitt said with a smile.

"Yes, but which specific touchdown?" Gordo said.

"There have been a lot of special ones," Emmitt said. "But my favorite was the first one I scored in the NFL. It was against Washington, I remember. Another favorite was the one I scored last year to set the NFL record with twenty-five touchdowns in one season."

"Is it true that you keep all the footballs when you score?" asked another camper.

"That's right. I've got all of them, from my days at the University of Florida to today. I've given some away to special friends, and I keep the rest at my card store in Florida."

"Can I get one next year, Emmitt?" Jenna asked.

"We'll see," Emmitt said. "First I've got to score some touchdowns!"

Troy laughed and slapped his teammate on the back. "Emmitt, you could score a touchdown in your sleep," he said. "You know what he calls it when we move the team inside the twenty-yard line? He says, 'Now we're in the Emmitt Zone!' "

"Is that true, Emmitt?" Jenna asked.

"The Emmitt Zone is a place where all things

are possible," Emmitt said. "I love being in the Emmitt Zone."

"Maybe that's what they should call it instead of the end zone," said Rusty. "That would be cool!"

"Then what would the other guys who scored say?" asked Emmitt. "It's their end zone, too."

"Except when you have the ball, Emmitt," Troy said.

Cookie finally brought out the trays of pizzas. The first dozen pizzas were gone faster than lightning in the sky over the prairie.

Gordo began to eat his third piece, but he stopped suddenly. A giant green, gooey blob was sizzling in the middle of his slice. It glistened in the light. What was it? It didn't look like anything Gordo had ever seen!

He yelled and dropped the slice back onto his plate. "Ahhhh! What the heck is that?"

Cookie looked over from where he was serving some other campers. "What's the matter, city slicker? Haven't you ever had cactus pizza?"

Four other kids who were chewing on slices of cactus pizza all suddenly spit it out. "Cactus pizza!" Gordo yelled. "What are you trying to do? Poison us? Or spike the insides of our mouths with thorns?"

"Quit your yapping, you crazy colt," laughed Cookie. "Nothing wrong with cactus. I use it in salads and in chili and, of course, on pizza. It's delicious!"

Gordo looked uncertainly at the slice on his plate. He'd never eaten cactus before. He poked it with his finger. It was sort of semi-smushy, like a banana. He sniffed it.

Finally, he took a small bite. "Hey," he said. "Hey, this is okay!"

"No kidding," Cookie said. "Would I serve you something that didn't taste good?"

Before Fats could speak up and tell about the time Cookie mixed up the sugar and salt and made the world's first dessert chili, Cookie interrupted him. "Don't say a word, Fats! That chili was a mistake!"

The group plowed through pizza after pizza. After a while, Fats laughed and then looked over at Rusty. "Say, Red, how many slices have you eaten?"

"This is my fourth piece, stickman," said Rusty triumphantly, holding up what was left of his cactus pizza.

"Well, I hope you know how to sing," Fats laughed. "Remember our bet? This is my eighth piece. You owe me a song."

The rest of the campers laughed as Rusty glowered at Fats. "Sing, Rusty, sing," they said.

"All right, fella, loosen up them pipes," Fats laughed. "Let's hear it good and loud."

Rusty stood up and glared at Fats. And he began to sing . . . really badly.

"Hoooome on the NFL field, where the Bears and the Patriots play . . ."

"Hey, that's not right," Fats yelled.

"Let me finish," answered Rusty with a smile. He kept singing, louder this time. "Where seldom is heard a non-Super Bowl word, and Dallas wins every Sunnnnday!" The whole room, especially Troy and Emmitt, burst out in applause. Rusty smiled at Fats. *That'll teach him,* he thought.

After they finished eating and helped Cookie clean the cook tent, the campers returned to the bus to grab their backpacks. On the way to the bus, the three friends talked with the other campers. They discovered that few of the campers were great riders like they were.

The sun was going down when they walked through camp toward their bus. The sky was painted with streaks of orange and red and yellow. The hills outside camp were getting darker and darker as the sky changed colors. Behind them, the kids could see stars begin to blink in the evening sky. It had been a long day.

First there was the long, boring morning spent on the bus, then the excitement of meeting Troy and Emmitt. There was also the wild stampede and the "ghost" that turned out to be Cookie.

Now it was time to hit the bunkhouse and get some shut-eye, as the cowboys would say.

They made it to the front of the bus, only to find the door wide open. "I could have sworn I closed it after the bus driver took my car back into town," Shorty said.

"Well, that just means I can get to sleep faster," Rusty said. He bounded up the stairs to grab his stuff. Then he stopped suddenly at the top of the stairs.

His mouth dropped open and he pointed slowly out in front of him.

"Wow!" he said. "Wow!"

"What is it, Rusty?" Gordo asked. He and Jenna were pushed onto the bus by the crowd of campers behind them.

Then all three of them stood in amazement as they looked at the inside of their bus.

Someone — or something — had been there before them. The inside of the bus was a total mess. It looked like it had been hit by a tornado!

9

Everything inside of the bus was thrown around like a defensive team's players after one of Emmitt's runs. There were clothes everywhere. Backpacks had been torn open and books, GameBoys, and footballs were tossed all over the seats. One of Rusty's T-shirts was tied to the steering wheel. Another was stuffed inside Gordo's thermos.

"This ghost guy has gone too far," Rusty yelled. He untied his shirt from the wheel and threw it to the ground in anger.

Shorty and Troy and Emmitt crowded into the bus after the kids.

Troy let out a low whistle. "Now what do you think happened here?"

The rest of the campers filed silently onto the bus. They headed toward their seats to see what they could find. After looking around where she had been sitting, Jenna finally found her bag wedged under a seat five rows away. She carefully opened it up and then let out a sudden cry. "Darn!" she yelled.

In the silent bus, everyone looked at her. "Sorry," she said. "But look what the ghost did here!" She held up two pieces of an autographed photo of Emmitt.

"I think we can find a way to replace that," said Emmitt from the front of the bus.

Jenna was upset, but she smiled back at Emmitt. "Thanks, Emmitt, that would be great!" she said.

The campers continued sorting through the mess. Troy and Emmitt and Shorty pitched in. Eventually everyone found their own stuff.

Nothing was missing, it turned out. Everything was just scattered all over the place. Gordo found a pair of his underwear in a compartment under the driver's seat. And Jenna's spare jeans were rolled up in the vent in the ceiling.

Then, when Rusty moved a towel hanging on the back wall of the bus, he screamed! He'd found something else . . . something that hadn't been there before.

On the wall over the seat he and Gordo and Jenna had been sitting on earlier that day, someone — or something — had written a message.

The letters were liquidy and dark red, and some of them had long drips running down from them.

GO AWAY!

10

E veryone stared at the dripping letters.
"Is that what I think it is?" Jenna asked
nervously.

"Back up, back up!" yelled Shorty, scrambling
toward the back of the bus. "Don't touch it!"

The campers moved into the seats to clear the
aisle for Shorty. He stopped when he reached the
back bench seat.

"This is too much," he said to no one in par-
ticular. "This is just way too much!"

He sniffed the air. Then, he reached out and
put his finger in the wet letter G!

"Ewww!" the campers said. "Gross! Don't
touch it!"

Then, as the kids on the bus watched in shock,
Shorty touched his finger to his tongue.

"Ahhh, Shorty, no!" Gordo said. "You don't
know what that is!"

"Yes, I do," Shorty said. "It's chili. And it
needs salt."

The tension left the bus like air leaving a balloon. "I guess this mysterious ghost doesn't carry a pen," Shorty laughed. But to Jenna, his eyes looked troubled. *He's just trying to make us feel better,* she thought. *This guy is really scared of something.*

And he wasn't the only one!

They finished gathering up their belongings, and then everyone went into the bunkhouse. There was one bed for each camper in two long rows along the walls.

The mess on the bus had been the last straw. Everyone in camp was exhausted and finally they decided to hit the sack, even though it was just after nine. As Jenna, Rusty, and Gordo climbed into their bunks, they whispered together.

"This place is giving me the creeps," Gordo said.

"Yea, but we're hangin' with the real-life Cowboys!" Rusty said.

"I don't know what to do," Jenna said. "Should I be happy I'm with them at a cool camp? Or should I be scared of some ghost I don't even believe in?"

Gordo yawned. "Well, I know what I'm going to try to do."

"What?" asked Jenna and Rusty.

Gordo answered with a snore. He was already asleep.

Rusty and Jenna fell asleep soon after. Rusty dreamed of a giant, ghostly white cowboy riding across the plains. He came closer and closer. The horse the ghost rode was becoming louder and louder. Its giant hooves crashed into rocks and boulders, smashing them to bits.

BANG! BANG! BANG!

The horse kept coming. Rusty was standing right in his path. He'd be crushed!

BANG! BANG! BANG!

Suddenly, Rusty shot out of bed like a jack-in-the-box. There was no horse. It had just been a dream.

Then, amazingly, the noise came again.

BANG! BANG! BANG!

Rusty looked around in terror. He saw a figure at the doorway, a dark shadow outlined by the dawn's early light.

Rusty was scared. Some dreams you don't want to come true. Had the ghost from his dream come to get them?

11

The shadowy figure stepped into the room.

It was Shorty, banging two garbage lids together.

BANG! CRASH! SMASH!

"Let's go! Let's go! Up and at 'em!" he yelled.

Troy and Emmitt followed Shorty in shouting and yelling at the top of their lungs. "Rise and shine, buckaroos!" they called. "Time to hit the trail!"

Now the entire bunkhouse was wide awake. How could they not be with all that noise?

"Can't we sleep in a little bit?" Rusty asked, relieved it wasn't the ghost. He looked out the window. "The sun is barely up."

"Cowboys start their days early, son," Shorty said. "Grab your boots and let's get some grub."

The Dallas Cowboys led the junior cowboys out to the cook tent, where Cookie had obviously been hard at work. Before he served up trays of eggs and sausage and pancakes and granola, Shorty called for quiet.

"Folks, I got an announcement and a problem," the one-eyed man said. "We have to change the schedule a bit. There's a big storm heading this way, about a day or so out. And I've got a small herd of cattle chewing on a new pasture a half-day's ride away. We can't leave them alone in the storm.

"Right now, there's only a pair of wranglers, Junior and Romario, watching all those cattle. They can't bring them in alone. Fats, Troy, and I have to go help bring the herd in. You campers will have to stay here with Cookie."

"Hey, what about me?" asked Emmitt. "I can ride pretty well. We've got so many Texans on our football team that they've been showing me how for years."

"Okay," Shorty said. "I guess we're one short. Rex must have been spooked away by that bus-wrecking ghost. I can't find him anywhere. So I guess we can use the help. Emmitt, you can come with us, too, but . . ."

Jenna stood up. *I didn't take the world's longest bus ride to hang out with a cook,* she thought. "We're coming, too!" she said, and pulled Gordo and Rusty to their feet next to her. "We can ride as well as anyone!"

Shorty looked at her. A smile parted his whiskery chin. "Well, cowgirl, ya got some

48

spunk, I'll give you that," he said. "You say you can ride? Okay! We'll just see about that. After breakfast, come to the corral to get your mounts."

The three friends high-fived each other. The rest of the campers weren't too psyched about staying behind, but none of them was good enough on a horse yet. Maybe next year.

"Eat up, y'all," Cookie called as he dished up breakfast. "You've got a long day of ridin' ahead of you. You're gonna need all the energy you can get to fight that ghost!" Cookie cackled and giggled as he dished up the eggs.

"I'm telling you, Rusty," Gordo said. "That guy is weird."

"I hope he didn't get that way eating cactus," Rusty replied. "Look, it's in the eggs, too!" He pointed out the flecks of green stuff that were sprinkled in the scrambled eggs.

"At least I hope it's cactus," he added with a grimace.

The campers polished off their breakfast quickly, then gathered by the horse corral to meet their mounts. By tomorrow afternoon, they'd be heading back into camp with the herd. It would be a real cattle drive.

First, though, they had to meet their horses. Since Jenna, Rusty, and Gordo all had done some riding before, they got spirited horses.

Shorty showed each of the three to his or her

horse. He told them to wait for instructions before they got on. Fats, Troy, and Emmitt were already on their horses and waiting just outside the corral entrance while Shorty spoke.

"Okay, cowboys," he began. "Now you're with your best friend on the range — your horse. He'll take you where you want to go, if you know how to tell him. I know you cowpokes have ridden before, but here's a refresher. A little heel kick to get them started, then use the reins to guide them left or right. Pull back a bit on the reins to make 'em stop. We won't be doing much hard riding today, just a long walk."

Rusty, who was a great rider, said, "Darn. I was hoping for a real gallop."

"Maybe later this week, pardner," Shorty said. "Remember always get on a horse from his left side. Sit up nice and straight, and keep your feet in the stirrups. That's about it. Let's walk our horses out to the corral entrance and get saddled up!"

Everyone grabbed their horses' reins and began leading them out to the corral gate. Gordo was near the front of the group.

As he got near the corral gate, his horse suddenly made a terrible sound. Gordo froze when he saw what had frightened his horse.

In the dirt in front of his feet, a giant rattlesnake reared its deadly head!

12

The rattler's tail shook while its head bobbed up and down. Gordo didn't move a muscle. His horse was backing away, straining the lead. The fierce snake bared its fangs and began to move toward him.

Before anyone could say a word or do a thing, Troy grabbed a football from his saddlebag and threw it. The ball smacked the rattler in the head. A perfect pass!

Gordo finally could move. He was scared, but he got his horse under control and moved away from the snake.

Meanwhile, Fats jumped from his horse and pinned the stunned snake with his boot. He picked up the snake carefully and carried it away.

Shorty laughed. "I guess we'll have some snake meat for dinner tonight," he said. But no one else was laughing.

"Thanks, Troy," Gordo said. "I didn't know what to do." He was still shaking a bit.

"You did the right thing, Gordo," Troy said. *"You hung tough!"*

Gordo smiled.

The campers went on getting on their horses. As they passed by Shorty at the corral entrance, he checked to make sure their saddles were on tight and their feet were in the stirrups. He also introduced each rider to his or her horse.

"Jenna, you're on Red Velvet," he said. "Gordo, your horse is Brains."

"That makes sense," laughed Rusty. "What's my horse's name?"

"Well, young fella, you're such a big mouth, you got the toughest horse," Shorty said. He winked at Troy and Emmitt. "You're riding Dynamite!"

"Dynamite!" yelled Rusty. "Yikes!" He grabbed the horse tighter with his legs. "What kind of name is that?"

Shorty laughed again. "He's perfectly safe. But ya gotta be real nice to him. He's got a temper!"

The riders filed out of camp single file. Fats was in the lead on Bones, a horse almost as skinny as he was. Shorty was riding a mule named Dallas and bringing up the rear. Jenna, Rusty, and Gordo rode near Troy and Emmitt.

"Hey, Troy," Rusty called out. "What's your horse's name?"

"Spiral," Troy said.

"Just like one of your passes," Rusty yelled.

"Well, most of the time anyway," Troy answered. "Hey, Emmitt! Did you know you're riding Touchdown?"

"You bet," Emmitt called back. "It sounded like a good idea!"

"Emmitt and Touchdown!" Rusty laughed. "Now that's the way it should be!"

The line of cowboys continued on into the desert. The camp disappeared slowly behind them.

As they rode along, no one thought about the ghost. There was too much to see and do on the trail.

Rusty remembered their bus ride yesterday morning. He thought there was nothing out here. But now, up close and moving more slowly, he saw all sorts of cool things. A lizard was sunning itself on a rock. A patch of wildflowers had sprung up next to a tall cactus plant. The rocks and sand were all shades of brown, red, yellow, and orange. The tumbleweeds looked like bouncing footballs, rolling this way and that while pushed by the wind. *There's something out here, after all*, he thought.

Gordo wasn't as good a rider as his pals, so he concentrated on following their horses. He was glad Jenna had spoken up, but he was a little nervous.

He didn't see as much as Rusty saw. He was just watching the back of Brains' head. The dark brown mane switched back and forth, back and forth as he walked. Sometimes he'd step on a rock and Gordo would have to stay balanced as the horse leaned slightly to one side. Gordo also watched the cracked leather of the saddle as it shifted a bit on the horse's back. He looked up once in a while to make sure there was a horse in front of him. He tried to keep the lead rider lined up between Brains' ears.

Jenna was behind Gordo. Her horse was a rich red color, a roan, it was called. She was a good natural rider. She knew how to stay balanced, how to shift with the horse as it walked, how to hold the reins firmly, but not too tightly. She was such a good athlete that controlling her body was easy. She divided her concentration between the beautiful Texas scenery and her horse.

After about a couple hours of riding, they were all beginning to get sore. Shorty led them to a shady spot at the bottom of a small cliff.

"Okay," he called out. "You can all climb down and rest a spell."

Everyone climbed stiffly down from their horses. Rusty and Gordo rubbed their butts. "Man, don't you have any padded saddles?" Rusty asked.

"Sorry, pardner," Shorty said. "The only

padding you get is what you bring with you wherever you sit!"

Gordo pointed farther up the trail, where the cliff met a pile of rocks. There was a dark patch amid the orange-red cliff face. "What's up there, Shorty?"

"That's one of the caves Troy was telling you about, the ones that make the wind sing. They say that's the home of the Lost Cowboy Ghost!"

Troy and Emmitt walked over to listen. "Now, Shorty, you cut that out," Emmitt said. "You're just scaring the kids."

"Just scaring you, you mean," Troy teased.

"I'm not scared," Emmitt said forcefully. "I'm just not sure."

"Why don't we go up there to find out?" Rusty asked.

"I think we should all just stay here," Fats said. "We don't know what's in there and we can't have anyone falling down a shaft!"

"Fats is right, Rusty," Shorty said. "Let's all stay together."

Rusty said he would, but he still wanted to check it out.

After everyone had had a short rest, they saddled up and headed out again. As they passed the cave, Rusty pulled Dynamite to a stop and let the others pass him. As Shorty reached him,

Rusty said, "I forgot my canteen, Shorty, can I go back and get it?"

"Off you go, fella," Shortly answered. "But hurry back." He continued on to catch up to the group.

But Rusty wasn't going back to the rest stop. He was going to the cave of the Lost Cowboy Ghost.

He guided Dynamite over there, and climbed down as he got nearer. The giant black hole of the cave entrance looked like nighttime. He couldn't see anything inside.

But in the dust just outside the entrance, he saw something.

A piece of metal was shining in the sunlight. He reached down and picked it up. It was a coin, a U.S. silver dollar.

Rusty brushed off the dirt that coated the coin. He held it up close to read the faded writing. And he almost dropped the dollar in shock!

The date on the coin was 1875 . . . the same year the Lost Cowboy Ghost disappeared!

13

Rusty shook his head in disbelief. *This can't be,* he thought. This would be too much of a coincidence. A ghost disappears in 1875 and a coin with that date appears!

He looked into the darkness of the cave. *Does the ghost live here?* He decided to go in for a quick look. He tied Dynamite's reins to a rock. Then he took his first steps into the lair of the Lost Cowboy Ghost.

Rusty's footsteps echoed in the cave entrance. He could hear water rushing somewhere ahead. The air was cool and moist in the cave, and he felt a bizarre chill run through him. There was something in there, and he could feel it. He took a few more tentative steps. Then he thought, *This is crazy.* He couldn't see a thing.

Suddenly, the prairie wind whipped up and the eerie singing of the rocks began again. The noise filled the cave and rattled Rusty's eardrums! He felt like he had his head in a stereo speaker.

Forget this, he said to himself. He ran out of the cave entrance and quickly climbed on top of Dynamite. Digging his sneakers into the horse's muscular side, he took off.

As he rode away, the singing died away behind him. But he spurred Dynamite on faster and faster anyway. *Let the other guys walk their horses*, he thought, as the wind whipped his red hair. *I'm gonna ride!*

He was really a cowboy, galloping across the plains! He imagined he was chasing bank robbers, or riding for the Pony Express. This was just like the movies!

And in his right hand, he clutched the mysterious coin tightly. *Wait until they see this*, he thought.

Dynamite's hooves clomped over and over on the dusty ground, *tha-dump, tha-dump, tha-dump*. Rusty could see the group appear as small figures ahead of him. He began to slow Dynamite to a canter, and then to a walk.

Reaching Shorty, he held out his hand.

"Hey, Shorty!" Rusty called. "Get a load of this."

"Sounds like you found more than your canteen, fella," Shorty said.

"I sure did," Rusty said breathlessly. "I found a coin that belonged to the Lost Cowboy Ghost."

Shorty pulled alongside Rusty. The redhead's wind-whipped hair was pointing in every direction, and his shirt was covered with dust. But he was wearing a smile as wide as his face.

"Let's see what you got, son," Shorty said.

Rusty held out his right hand triumphantly, palm up.

"There's nothing there," said Shorty.

Rusty looked down at his hand in a panic. All that was left in his palm was a handful of dust! The coin had crumbled! Now he had no evidence of the ghost!

"It was there, I swear," Rusty yelled. "I found a coin from 1875! It had to be his. The ghost's, I mean. I must have dropped it."

"Well, I don't know what you found," Shorty said. "But I know what we've got to find — my cattle." With that, he turned his horse and trotted forward to rejoin the other campers.

Rusty threw the dust onto the ground. He looked back at the cliff face where he'd found the coin outside the cave. "There's something in there," he said. "I know I found that coin!" He spurred Dynamite softly and the horse walked onward.

When Rusty caught up to the group, he rode ahead to meet up with Jenna and Gordo. "Did Shorty tell you what I found?" Rusty asked.

"Yeah," laughed Jenna. "In the middle of a huge desert, he said you discovered sand!" She and Gordo laughed so hard they almost fell off their horses.

"Very funny, you guys, very funny," Rusty said. "But I'm telling you, I found a coin from 1875."

"Well, where did you spend it out here?" Gordo asked. He pretended to look all around him, searching for something. "I don't see a McDonald's anywhere." Jenna laughed again.

"You're too much, Rusty," she said between fits of laughing. "First the ghost was Cookie, now the ghost is walking around the desert with a hole in his pocket."

"What's next, Rusty?" Gordo asked. "Horses flying across the sky?"

Rusty sulked back into line as his friends kept laughing. *I'll show them,* he thought. *There's something here . . . and I'm going to find it!*

Troy and Emmitt watched Gordo and Jenna tease Rusty about his "discovery."

Troy slowed his horse to let Rusty catch up to him. "Don't let them bug you, Rusty," Troy said. "They're just having a little fun. They aren't being mean."

"I know, Troy," Rusty said. "But I also know what I found."

"Rusty, I have a feeling this game is just getting started," Troy said. "And you've got to make sure to be ready for the fourth quarter. You might just win this thing yet!"

Rusty smiled, finally, and thanked Troy for helping out.

As Troy walked his horse ahead to talk to another camper, Rusty just shook his head. *That was Troy Aikman,* he thought. He'd been hanging with Troy for a whole day now, but it was still too wild to believe. Seems like there were a lot of things hard to believe about Shorty's Six Points Ranch!

About an hour later, they came to a watering hole. It was just a wide place in a little trickle of a stream, but it was a good place to give the horses a drink. And for the campers to have some lunch.

After everyone had dismounted and led his or her horse to water, the campers and the NFL stars sat under the shade of the lone tree at the watering hole. Cookie had packed brown bag lunches for everyone. Before they left the camp, Shorty had made sure everyone put their lunch in their saddlebag. He also had brought a pair of big water jugs.

"Drink up, everyone," Shorty said. "Don't waste a drop. Water is the most valuable thing out here on the plains. That stream is okay for horses, but you city folks would get sick if you drank that. So stick with what I brought."

Gordo was last in line for the water. He filled his cup and went back to his horse to get his lunch. As he reached in to his bag, he felt a cool wind blow across the camp. It wasn't the singing wind, this was different. Although they had been riding all morning in the hot sun, Gordo suddenly felt cold.

But that doesn't make any sense, he thought. He ignored the wind and reached for this sandwich.

Ack! It moved!

Gordo yanked his hand out from the bag with a start. There was something in his saddlebag! Something alive!

14

Gordo carefully peered over the edge of the saddlebag. Was it another snake?

As he looked over the rim of the deep leather pouch, he heard a soft little sound. Then he reached in and pulled out Cookie's kitten!

The little cat had a mouth full of bread and there were scraps of brown paper in its claws. "That cat is eating my lunch," Gordo cried. Then he thought, *What are we going to do with a kitten in the middle of a cattle drive?*

He pulled what was left of his food out of the bag and returned the kitten to its nest. Gordo even left it a bit more bread to eat.

Gordo went back under the tree to join the others. He was grumbling as much as his stomach was. And now he had only part of a sandwich left over. *This is going to be a long afternoon*, he thought . . . *and a hungry one.*

Emmitt saw Gordo sulking by the tree and came over. "Here, Gordo, have some of my sandwich," he said. "I brought too much anyway."

Gordo looked up at Emmitt. "That would be great, Emmitt, thanks," Gordo said with a smile. He took half of the enormous submarine sandwich from the superstar running back.

"Us Cowboys gotta stick together, right?" Emmitt said.

"That's right!" Gordo said. "So tell me, what's tougher, making a cattle drive or trying to score a touchdown?"

Emmitt finished a bite of sandwich and thought about the question. "They're both pretty hard," he said. "I'd wouldn't mind having a horse while I'm going through the line. But on the other hand, these cows are even bigger than Reggie White!"

Gordo laughed while he imagined Emmitt riding across the football field on his horse Touchdown, carrying the ball with one hand and holding the reins with the other.

Emmitt continued. "I'm having a lot of fun riding the range out here, but I'd still rather be playing football. A cattle drive takes days. A football game only lasts a few hours."

While Gordo, Emmitt, and the others finished their lunches, Shorty stood up to tell them what they'd be doing that afternoon.

"These cows have to get home, and they're too dumb to know the way," Shorty said. "It's sort of like taking your baby sister or brother out to the store. You can't leave 'em alone. And you've got to make sure they're safe. That's the cowboy's job — keep his cattle safe.

"I could see this morning that you all ride well. You've all got experienced horses, too, so they'll know what to do. But you've got to tell them when to do it. When you see a cow wandering out of the group, just ride up next to it and it will move back into the herd. If it doesn't move right away, give it a big yell. And if it takes off, you'll have to lasso it back into the group. The two most important things you have to guide the cows home are your voice and your rope."

Rusty remembered how Troy had lassoed the stunt cow in the classroom. He hoped he could do the same. So far that morning he'd missed every cactus he'd tried to rope on the way to the watering hole. Then he wondered, *Can you lasso a ghost?*

Shorty kept talking. "Let's practice our cow-calling yells. Everybody say 'Heeee-yah!' "

The three Dallas campers and the two Dallas Cowboys all screamed "heeee-yah!" at the top of their lungs. "Not bad," Shorty said. "Not bad at all. You just might make it as cowboys yet."

Shorty paired off everyone. "No cowboy works alone in my outfit," he said.

Emmitt asked to ride with Gordo. Jenna and Troy became a team. "Rusty," Shorty said, "you ride with Fats."

Rusty was bummed. His friends got Dallas Cowboys, he got a skinny cowboy.

"*Mi amigo*, Rusty," Fats said. "*¡Vámanos!* Let's go!" And he took off at a gallop.

Rusty spurred Dynamite and wheeled around to follow Fats. *That skinny cowboy might eat more pizza than me*, thought Rusty, *but he was going to have to go a ways to outride me.*

Emmitt and Gordo watched Fats and Rusty take off. Gordo looked nervously at Emmitt. "Um, do we have to do that, too?" he asked.

"Let's just take it easy, Gordo," Emmitt said. "I'm not exactly Bill Pickett on this horse."

"Who's Bill Pickett?" Gordo asked.

"He was one of the greatest rodeo stars of the early part of the century," Emmitt replied. "And the greatest African-American star, too."

Wow, thought Gordo. *That's actually something I didn't know.*

"Heeee-yah!" Gordo yelled. He checked to see that the saddlebag with the kitten inside was closed. Then he called out, "Let's ride!"

And they clopped off together to join the herd.

Troy looked over at Jenna. "Ready to go?"

"I've been ready for months," she said. "I can't believe I'm finally here."

"Well, believe it," Troy said. "It's time to be a cowboy!"

15

The cowboys headed across the plain to the big herd of cows waiting for them. As the riders got closer, they saw the huge cloud of dust that the cows were kicking up.

"It looks like a big brown traffic jam," Jenna said.

"Man, that's a lot of cows," Rusty added.

They were looking down from a small rise at a sea of cows. Big cows, small cows, medium cows, all mooing and snorting and clomping along. The noise rose up toward them . . . along with the smell.

"I wish I had a cold," Gordo said.

"Why would you wish that?" Emmitt asked.

"Then I wouldn't be able to smell these things," Gordo said.

Fats and Rusty were already out helping to move the herd. The other two campers took up positions along the sides of the big rectangle of cows as it moved across the plain. Jenna noticed that no one rode ahead of the cows. If they decided to stampede, no one wanted to be in the way. *I know how that feels*, she thought.

Emmitt showed Gordo how to watch for stray cows. When one started wandering from the group, he rode alongside and guided it back with the others.

"You try it, Gordo," Emmitt called over the mooing of the cows. "There goes one now!"

Gordo gulped and spurred Brains forward a bit faster. They caught up to the big cow. As it walked along, it looked up at Gordo with big, brown eyes.

"Move over, cow," Gordo yelled. "Back with the others." *Eldrick Gordon, cattle traffic cop*, he thought.

The cow ignored him and kept walking away from the herd.

"NOW, COW!" Gordo yelled even louder.

At that the cow turned and headed back to the others. *Wow!* thought Gordo. *I did it. I'm a cowboy!*

Jenna and Troy were on the opposite side of the herd from Gordo and Emmitt. As they rode along, Jenna pulled her baseball cap (with the official Dallas Cowboys' star on it, of course) low over her eyes to keep out the sun. Troy did the same with his wide-brimmed ten-gallon hat.

They were riding side by side next to the

cows, enjoying the weather and the scenery and the fun of the drive.

A couple of cows drifted out of line ahead of Troy. Jenna was almost shocked out of her saddle when he barked out at them.

"Twenty-seven Red right, HUT, HUT, HUT!" he yelled.

The cows moved quickly back into line. *Being a quarterback can come in handy when you're herding cattle*, thought Jenna.

"Blue eighty-eight, Blue eighty-eight, HUT, HUT," she yelled at the cows.

"You'd make a great quarterback, Jenna," Troy said with a laugh. "Moving cows around is like giving signals to offensive linemen. Only cows probably don't eat as much as linemen!"

Jenna thought about how she'd look in an NFL uniform. She looked over at Troy. "Did you always want to be a quarterback, Troy?" she said.

"I always wanted to be an athlete, I knew that," Troy said. "I played a lot of sports when I was a kid. But football became my favorite. When I ended up at UCLA for college, and began to improve, I thought I might have a shot at making the NFL."

"Might have a shot?" Jenna said in surprise. "You've won three Super Bowls!"

"But that didn't just happen, Jenna," Troy said. "I have only been able to win all those games because of hard work and the skill of my teammates. I have responsibilities, sure, but it's a team game. No one just wakes up one morning and decides they're in the NFL. It takes practice to make it there."

Jenna thought of the times she had skipped her flag football team's practice. She just really loved the games, not the boring practices. "But the games are the best part!" she said.

Troy shifted in his saddle to look over at her. "Without practice, there wouldn't be any games," he said. "The only way you can improve at anything, and enjoy it more, is if you practice. You can't rely on just being a natural athlete."

Jenna and Troy rode on in silence. Ever since she was small, Jenna had been faster and stronger than a lot of the other kids. She hadn't worked at it, it had just happened. She began to wonder how good she could be if she worked even harder.

"Hey, Troy," she said finally. "Maybe later, we can practice some passing, okay?"

"Okay, Jenna," Troy said. "I'm always happy to practice passing."

The two new friends rode on together.

Rusty was learning something, too: Riding at the back of a herd of cows was not the cleanest thing in the world.

"Yeah, I know," Fats said. "This isn't the most glamorous cowboy job, but it's *muy importante*. The slowest and smallest cows always end up at the back . . . and the coyotes know that. We're here to make sure all the cows make it back, no matter how small or slow they are."

Rusty still wanted to be up front with Gordo, Jenna, and the Dallas Cowboys. He felt as if he had been stuck back here in no-man's land. All the dust the cows kicked up was blowing back at them. He had had to put a handkerchief over his mouth, like Fats had done. And he still felt like he was eating sand.

"Why can't one of the other cowboys do this?" Rusty asked.

"This was Rex's job for the last few drives we've had, but I guess he's chickened out, too."

"So how come we get stuck with it?" Rusty asked. "This job is no fun."

"Just because a job's no fun doesn't mean it's not worth doin'," Fats said. "We're just as important to this drive as them fellers at the front."

Rusty grumbled a bit more. *Nothing's going to happen back here,* he thought. *This is boring.*

Just then he saw Fats stand up in the saddle and point at something near the back of the herd.

Rusty watched the skinny cowboy spur his

horse forward at a gallop. "C'mon, Rusty!" Fats yelled.

Rusty looked ahead to where Fats was riding. Two fierce-looking animals were racing toward the cattle from behind a stand of cactus.

Coyotes!

16

*W*hoa! *This might not be so boring, after all,* thought Rusty. He yelled at Dynamite, "Heeeee-yah!" and poked his heels into the big horse's side. Dynamite dug his hooves into the sand and took off at a gallop.

As he rode, Rusty could see the dusty gray coyotes ahead of him moving toward a calf at the back of the pack. The calf's mother suddenly whirled and charged at the oncoming coyotes. Rusty watched as she whacked first one coyote, then another, with her horns. But the coyotes just kept coming.

Fats reached the battle and grabbed something from a bag hanging from his saddle horn. They were rocks! He flung one after another toward the coyote. Finally, he got a bull's-eye, hitting the animal square on the back. It yelped and took off for the brush.

Fats began to chase it away. "Get the other

one, Rusty," he yelled over his shoulder. "But stay on your horse!"

Rusty didn't know what to do. He guided Dynamite to where the coyote was still stalking the calf. The predator was keeping far away from the mother cow's horns. But it was quicker than the big cow and was trying to circle around her to get the calf. The herd had moved quickly ahead and was getting farther and farther away. Fats was on his way back, but he was still about a hundred yards from Rusty.

Rusty was alone with the coyote and the two cows he was supposed to protect. It was up to him.

How am I going to stop a coyote? thought Rusty. *I've got nothing to throw at it, like Fats did.*

He moved Dynamite closer and yelled at the top of his lungs.

"Scram!" he shouted at the coyote. "Take off! Get outta here!"

But the coyote just bared his sharp teeth and growled.

Then Rusty remembered his lasso. It was coiled into a loop on the side of his saddle. He quickly reached down and grabbed it. He took the loop of the lasso and spun it over his head, just like he'd seen Troy do. Rusty hadn't been able to make any of his practice throws, but there was no time for practice now! He just had to make it to save the calf.

The coyote was just feet away from the frightened calf. Rusty kept twirling the rope and then took careful aim at the coyote. He threw the lasso!

The rope zinged out over the ten yards between the coyote and Dynamite.

It flew right over the coyote's head!

Rusty was stunned. Now what?

He yanked the rope back hard. Maybe if he pulled the rope back fast, he'd have enough time to try again before the coyote got the calf. But as Rusty was pulling, he snapped the end of the rope like a whip. The rope flicked up and whacked the coyote on the snout! The animal turned away from the calf to growl again at Rusty and Dynamite.

Uh-oh! thought Rusty. *I've saved the calf, but now I'm in trouble. First a ghost that isn't there and now a coyote that is!*

But Rusty's teammate came through to save the day. Not Fats, though. Dynamite!

The horse charged at the coyote as Rusty held on to the reins for dear life. Dynamite kicked out at the coyote with his front legs. The coyote took off!

It ran after its partner and disappeared into the brush, just as Fats came back to help.

"Looks like you two handled yourself all right there," Fats said as Rusty coiled up his rope and patted Dynamite on the neck. *"Muy bueno, amigo.* You saved the day!"

"And I thought I'd be bored back here," Rusty said. He reached across to shake Fats' hand. *Wait until I tell Gordo and Jenna,* Rusty thought. *They'll have to believe me this time!*

The cattle drive continued all afternoon. Working together, they herded the cows back in the direction of the Six Points Ranch. The Lost Cowboy Ghost was far from their minds as they worked the herd like real cowboys.

Gordo became an expert at guiding strays back into the herd. He just moved Brains next to the cow and they walked together back into the crowd.

Jenna was getting hoarse from all the yelling she was doing, but she was having a great time. Barking signals with Troy Aikman out here on the prairie. *Not bad,* she thought, *not bad at all.*

And Rusty was becoming a rope expert. With a little help from Fats, he began to snare whatever he aimed at with his lasso. First he roped a cactus, then a cow. He only snagged one of the horns the first time, but it was enough to slow the trotting cow until Fats could ride up and guide it back in. After a few more tries, Rusty thought he was getting as good with a rope as Troy was with a football!

As they rode on, the cliff they'd passed earlier — the one with the mysterious cave — came closer and closer on the horizon ahead.

Rusty stopped for a moment to wipe the dust out of his eyes. He looked up at the cliff, a mile or so away. There was something moving on top of the cliff!

He spurred Dynamite forward, keeping one eye on the cliff and one eye on where he was going. He had to get to Jenna or Gordo. He was tired of not being believed!

The figure on the cliff seemed to glide back and forth. *It's almost hovering,* Rusty thought. *That's no coyote!* Then he got a better look at it. It was a man on a horse. A man he could almost see through!

He pulled up beside Jenna. "Look!" he said. "It's the ghost!"

Jenna reined in Red Velvet. "Yeah, right, Rusty!" she said. "Has he come looking for his lost money? Or did he want to tell us to go away again?"

"I'm telling you, that's him," Rusty cried. "Just look up there."

With a shrug, Jenna looked toward where Rusty's finger pointed.

Her mouth dropped open and she let out a

small yelp. Troy looked over to see what was the matter.

The three cowboys looked up together at the top of the cliff.

As they watched, the Lost Cowboy Ghost reared up his horse and flew off the edge of the cliff! He was heading straight for them. They had to duck their heads as he soared past, laughing.

His skin and his clothes and his horse were grayish-white. As he got closer, they could see his face. There was nothing but a skull in a cowboy hat!

The ghost hovered for a moment over the trio. They looked up in fear at the laughing skull. And then it spoke to them.

"Has any of you seen my calf?" it said with a hollow voice. It laughed fiendishly. And then it disappeared.

Poof! — as if it never had been there.

17

Rusty was scared and psyched at the same time. "See," he said to Jenna. "I told you there was something out here."

Then he stopped. And he was suddenly more frightened than he had realized. "Aaahh! I just saw a ghost!" he yelled. His screams frightened Dynamite, and the horse tried to run. But Rusty got control and slowed down the bucking beast.

Jenna was shaking in her saddle. The image of the skull was painted on her brain. "Did you see it, Troy?" Jenna asked.

"I-I-I'm not sure what I saw, Jenna," Troy stammered. "Was that a skull? And was he flying?"

"That's what I saw, too," Jenna said. "Looks like those cowboys that left the camp had a reason to be scared. That was horrible!"

Shorty, Gordo, and Emmitt heard the commotion and saw the others gathered in a small group. They rode over to see what was up.

"He was here!" Rusty shouted. "He was really here. The Lost Cowboy Ghost almost took our heads off!"

Jenna and Rusty talked over one another trying to tell Gordo and the others what they had seen.

"He was huge — " Jenna started.

"And he had big, sharp teeth and — " Rusty said.

"And he had on this big cape and his horse had steam coming out of his mouth — " added Jenna.

"And he pointed his bony finger right at us!" Rusty said.

Troy held up both hands. "Now hold on!" he said calmly. "Take it easy, both of you. We saw something pretty darned weird, but let's not exaggerate!"

Jenna and Rusty paused to catch their breath.

"Well, whatever we saw," Rusty said, "it sure wasn't like anything I've ever seen."

"That much is true," Troy said. "Shorty, I'm sorry to say that maybe this Lost Cowboy Ghost doesn't want us around here."

Shorty scratched his beard the way he'd done when they first met. He looked around at the anxious faces looking at him. Then he looked at the big herd of cattle, mooing and moving slowly back toward camp.

"Folks, here's the way I see it," he said.

"There's still a whole bunch of us, and there's only one ghost. And then there's these here cattle. Now it's our job, spook or no spook, to make sure these cattle go home." He stopped and glared at each of them with his one eye. "And that's just what we're gonna do!"

He wheeled Dallas around and spurred his way back to the herd.

Troy looked around at his new teammates. "Well," he said. "You heard the man. Let's get back to work."

Rusty and Jenna turned to look back at the cliff where they'd first seen the Lost Cowboy Ghost. They knew they'd have to pass by it to get the cows home. But they also knew they had the Dallas Cowboys on their side. So they figured the odds were about even.

The sun was close to setting by the time they got the herd underway again. The visit by the ghost had cost them a lot of time. They would have to make camp on the prairie that evening and finish the drive in the morning.

Rusty and Jenna rode near each other.

"I'm not sure I want to spend a whole night out here," Jenna said.

They slowed their horses while Shorty and Fats helped Romario and Junior guide the herd into a dry riverbed where they'd stay for the night. The riders would camp on the rise above the cows, so they could keep watch over them by moonlight.

The western sky was glowing orange as they set up camp. Everyone broke out their bedrolls and found a soft place to put them. But first they made sure to move any rocks. There's nothing worse than spending a night in a sleeping bag with a rock poking you in the back.

Shorty started the big cook fire. Fats broke out some cans of beans and some loaves of bread. Emmitt passed out some candy bars he'd been hiding. "Man, now I know why you were always my favorite player," Jenna said with a mouth full of chocolate.

They munched by the fire on beans and bread and chocolate. The ghost seemed far away now in the warmth of the fire. They were with friends. They were with heroes.

Tomorrow, they would be back in the safety of the camp.

Now all they had to do was survive one night out on the open prairie.

While a ghost waited to get them while they slept.

18

After everyone had eaten their fill of beans and bread, Shorty assigned Fats, Romario, and Junior to overnight shifts watching the cows.

"We can't let them alone all night," Shorty said. "Those coyotes might be back."

"That ghost might be back, too," Fats said with a grin. "But I'm not afraid of him." As Fats said that, though, Rusty saw him look cautiously toward the cliffside home of the Lost Cowboy Ghost.

"I wish Rex hadn't run off," Shorty said. "I've only got three cowboys to stay up all night watching the cows. They'll be real tired tomorrow when we need them."

"Didn't Rex even leave a note?" Jenna asked.

"Just plumb took off," Shorty said. "His horse, too. But all his stuff is still back in the ranch hands' bunkhouse."

"He seemed sort of mean when we met him at the cook tent," Gordo said.

"Rex has always had an ornery streak," Shorty said. "I've had to warn him several times to shape up or ship out. But when he does his work, he's a good cowboy."

"Speaking of good cowboys," Troy said, "who's up for a little touch football?"

All the campers' hands shot up! Troy went to his saddlebag to get a ball. Emmitt found a patch of soft sand they could play in.

"We've only got time for a few plays before it gets too dark," Emmitt said. "But anytime you can play football is a good one."

Emmitt and Troy were captains and they picked teams. Troy chose Jenna and Gordo, while Emmitt picked Rusty.

"Throw it to me, Troy," Jenna said as they went into a huddle to hear the play.

"Nope," Troy said. Jenna's face fell. "You're going to have to throw it. You're the quarterback!"

Jenna smiled. "What should I do?" she asked.

"Take charge," Troy said. "Tell the players where you want them to go. Then look for an open receiver and fire the ball!"

Jenna felt great that Troy had such faith in her. She gave Troy and Gordo different ways to go out for a pass. They went to the line and waited for her call.

She barked out the signals just like she and Troy had been doing all afternoon. "HUT, HUT,

HIKE!" she yelled. And the ball zipped back toward her.

Jenna grabbed it on the laces and looked out over the field. She saw Gordo wide open. Rusty was defending Gordo, but he had fallen down. As Gordo waved his arms and shouted, Jenna looked away. She wanted to throw to Troy!

She saw him on the right and tossed the ball toward him. But Emmitt stepped in front of the pass and intercepted it! He ran toward her with the ball. She stood her ground, waiting to tag him. Emmitt got closer and closer. Jenna could see his eyes staring right at her. *Uh-oh,* she thought. *He's in the Emmitt Zone!*

He got a few steps closer, and Jenna reached out to tag him. Then suddenly he wasn't there! ZING! He was on the other side of her, spiking the ball and high-fiving his teammates!

How did he do that? Jenna wondered. Then she remembered. *Oh, yeah, he's Emmitt Smith!*

Troy came over to her and said, "Why didn't you throw to Gordo? He was wide open."

"I wanted to throw to you, Troy," Jenna said.

"You can't just throw to me because you want to, Jenna. A good quarterback has to throw to the player who can help the team. Emmitt was all over me. Always look for the open man!"

Jenna was sorry she had messed up. But Troy was right. She had been showing off.

The two teams played a little while longer.

With Emmitt's help, Rusty was becoming a great runner. He zigged and zagged like crazy and made some great runs.

Then Jenna's team got the ball one last time.

She faded back to pass. She looked left for Troy, but Emmitt was covering him. She looked over the middle. Nobody was open. Then she saw Gordo racing down the right side.

Jenna heaved the ball with all her strength. It flew through the twilight air into Gordo's hands! He ran in for the touchdown!

Troy ran over to give Jenna a high five. "Now that's what a quarterback does, Jenna! Great throw!"

Everyone was tired from their long day, but excited that they had played football with two NFL superstars. Now it was time to hit the hay.

As they walked back toward the campfire, Troy was tossing the ball in the air. "Hey Shorty," he called out. "Catch!"

Troy fired a perfect spiral toward Shorty. Shorty turned for the ball and put up his hands.

And the ball went right through them! He missed!

The football spun on toward the campfire. CLANG! It smashed into a pot of hot chocolate that Shorty was cooking.

The pot tipped over onto the fire. And with a noisy burst of steam, the fire went out! It suddenly got so dark, they could barely see each other a few feet away.

They were alone in pitch darkness on a vast prairie.

Or maybe they weren't alone. . . .

19

Nobody moved. They couldn't, because they couldn't see where they were going. The fire sizzled and steamed, the last hot coals going out.

Slowly, everyone's eyes got adjusted to the darkness. They began to see shapes around them. Then they could see faces in the moonlight. Finally, the dark shapes of the hills and cliffs around them stood out against the blue-black sky.

"Dang it, Troy!" Shorty yelled out of the darkness. "I was a quarterback coach, not a receiver coach!"

Troy laughed, trying to keep everyone calm. "Shorty, you've got hands of stone!"

"Once we get this fire lit and I can see you, I'll get even," Shorty said.

Walking carefully so they didn't trip, the campers and the NFL stars moved toward the glow of the matches Shorty was using to relight the fire. The wood and coals were wet, and he was having a hard time.

"This might take a while," Shorty said. "Troy and Emmitt, can you make sure everyone finds a seat around the campfire circle here? I think I have some flashlights, too. Once we're fired up again, we can have that hot chocolate."

Soon everyone had found a seat on the logs and rocks around the campfire circle.

"I sure hope that ghost doesn't come back now," Jenna said. "He might have us right where he wants us."

"I just can't get that skull out of my head," Rusty added.

"If you got your skull out of your head, none of your hats would fit," Gordo laughed.

"You know what I mean, Gordo," Rusty said. "I was talking about the skull of the ghost in the cowboy hat."

Jenna shook her head, trying to clear the picture away, too. "That was gross," she said. "I can't believe I really saw it." She shook slightly all over, from the chill night air and from fright.

"What you saw and what it was may be two different things," Gordo said. "No one has ever proven beyond a doubt that ghosts exist. I think we should go up there tomorrow and find this ghost ourselves."

"Have fun, Gordo," Rusty said. "See you back at camp, when you can fly in yourself. Maybe we'll see what your skull looks like in a cowboy hat!"

"I don't think so, Rusty," Gordo said. "I want to find that thing. We can do it, I know we can. We don't want Shorty to lose his camp."

"Right," Jenna said. "A bunch of kids going ghost-hunting — I don't think so, either."

"I think we could do it," Emmitt said. "Shorty was right. There's only one ghost and there's a whole team of us. I sure wouldn't want to face any opponent alone, but when I've got my team behind me, I'll take on anyone." He reached out to clap Gordo on the back, but in the darkness, he smacked Troy on the back of the head.

"Hey!" Troy said, rubbing his head. "Emmitt's right. As long as we stick together and help each other out, we can lick this ghost."

Rusty laughed. "Lick the ghost! Now that would be gross!"

"I wonder what a ghost would feel like?" Gordo asked. "Cotton candy?"

"How about a snowcone?" Jenna wondered. "Ghosts are probably cold."

"Maybe you wouldn't be able to touch him at all," Emmitt said.

"Sort of like you on a touchdown run," Jenna said.

They talked on and on about ghosts and football and cows and stuff. Finally, the campfire began to glow.

They grew quiet as they all watched the fire. They were thinking about ghost hunting and about their exciting first day as working cowboys.

All around them, they heard the sounds of the desert at night. A few birds called out on their way to their nests. A few bugs chirped and clicked. A light breeze sent some tumbleweeds clicking across the sand. The fire crackled. The horses, tied up nearby, stamped their feet once in a while. And in the distance, a coyote howled at the moon.

It's really beautiful out here, Jenna thought. *It's hard to believe there could be a ghost in the middle of this calm and peaceful place.*

While he listened to the night sounds of the desert, Gordo was thinking about ghost hunting. He was going over in his head all the things they had seen: the mysterious sightings by the cowboys who had left camp; the messy bus and the weird message. Had Rusty really found a coin? And finally, the skull-headed cowboy that Troy, Jenna, and Rusty had seen. Something was bugging Gordo about the whole thing.

Suddenly all the noise around them stopped. The birds and bugs were silent. The horses stopped stamping. And the wind seemed to die down in an instant.

Then, WHOOOSH! a giant wind came into camp. The wind blew sand in their eyes. It tore their hats off and twirled them around over their heads. The horses neighed loudly in fright.

And the fire went out again.

"Dang it," Shorty yelled over the noise of the wind. "This is getting ridiculous!"

The wind increased and they held onto each other to keep from being blown over. Another noise was heard over the wind. THUP-THUP-THUP, over and over and over.

The noise grew louder and louder. Something was coming closer and closer. THUP-THUP-THUP, over and over and over.

A huge dark shape blotted out the moon and part of the sky.

Then from the shape a blinding light flared!

What now? thought Rusty as he held onto a log. *First ghosts . . . now UFOs?*

20

The light came closer and closer. The noise and the wind got louder and louder.

Finally the light was coming straight at them, not from the sky, but from ground level. The wind began to die down. The mysterious noise began to soften, thup-thup-thup . . .

Someone — or something — stepped into the light. Whatever it was began to move toward them.

The edges of the thing's silhouette shimmered in the light. As the giant noise began to die down, they heard the crunch-crunch-crunch of boots on the dirt.

"Do ghosts wear shoes?" Gordo asked.

"Can ghosts walk?" Jenna said.

Emmitt shielded his eyes from the bright light. He squinted into the dark silhouette.

"Is that who I think it is?" Emmitt asked.

"I think I know who you mean," Troy said.

"And if it is, I'm going to pound him for scaring us like that."

"Who is it?" Rusty said. "Do you actually know this ghost?"

"That's no ghost," Emmitt said, standing. "It's Prime Time!"

And Deion Sanders walked from his helicopter into their camp.

"Prime Time!" all the campers shouted. "All right!" This was getting to be too much. *No one back at school will believe us*, thought Jenna.

The chopper's spotlight lit up the entire campground and everyone could see the superstar defensive back/wide receiver. He wore a bright silver leather vest and dark blue pants. His boots were made of some sort of lizard.

"What's up, you guys?" Deion said. "I landed back at that Six Points Ranch you told me about. I met some guy named Rookie who smelled like beef stew!"

"You mean Cookie," Emmitt said. "He had a little accident at dinner last night. But hey, Prime Time, welcome aboard!"

"Glad you could make it, Deion," Troy said. "We've had quite an experience out here. We sure can use your help."

Jenna, Rusty, and Gordo crowded around Troy and Emmitt. Rusty cleared his throat real loud. "Ahem," he said.

Jenna pulled on Troy's shirtsleeve. "Aren't you going to introduce us?"

"Of course," Troy said. "Deion, these here cowboys are Rusty, Jenna, and Gordo. They're big Dallas Cowboys fans, and they've become our good buddies."

None of the kids knew what to say. They were meeting Deion, and Troy was saying they were his good buddies.

Finally, Rusty spoke up. "Deion, wow, this is great, I mean really great — you're the best, man . . . you're so fast . . . the way you run and then dance — " He stopped, breathless.

"No, no," Deion said. "Don't stop. Keep talking. I like it!" He laughed. "Great to meet you guys. When Emmitt called last night on the cell phone from his car, I hustled up here to lend a hand. We teammates always stick together, right, Emmitt?" The three Dallas players all shook hands.

"Right, Deion!" Emmitt said. He introduced Prime Time to Shorty and the others.

"I know you didn't play for Dallas when I was a coach there," Shorty said. "But I sure remember watching you play against us, darn you. But hey, you're a Cowboy now. Glad you could join us . . . even if your entrance was a little dramatic."

"Sorry about that, Shorty," Deion said. "But I

wanted to find you as fast as I could and horses just aren't my style."

"Well, they have to be your style out here," Troy said. "Because that's the only way we're letting you get back! You may have choppered in, but you're riding out!" Jenna, Gordo, and Rusty laughed while Deion argued with Troy.

Finally, Troy won out. Deion went back to the chopper to get his gear. Gordo frowned as he watched it fly away. The noise of the helicopter wasn't scary now because he knew what it was.

"I don't know about this, Troy," Deion said. "I was expecting to at least sleep indoors."

"Find a soft spot, Prime Time," laughed Emmitt.

"And don't forget to look for rocks!" Gordo said.

Troy got in one last tease. "And snakes!"

At that Deion just burst out laughing. "This is just too much, man, just too much!"

Rusty looked at another one of his heroes. One thing he had learned in the past day is that they're people, too. You can talk to them just like you'd talk to your friends.

"If you think this is too much, Deion, wait until you hear what else is going on," Rusty said. "We're not alone out here!"

"What do you mean, Rusty?" Deion said.

"He's not talking about the cows, Deion," Jenna said.

"I mean the Lost Cowboy Ghost!" Rusty added.

"Now I know you're kidding," Deion said. "There's no ghost out here. There's no ghosts anywhere. There is nothing out here but tumbleweeds and cactus. That's all I saw on the flight in here."

Rusty, Gordo, and Jenna remembered their bus ride the day before . . . although it seemed longer ago than that.

"That's what we thought when we rode in, too," Rusty said. "But things aren't always what they seem."

After Shorty got the fire started again, everyone took a seat around it. The kids told Deion about all the weird things that had been happening. Shorty told him about the cowboys who had deserted the camp. Troy wrapped it all up by describing the skull-headed cowboy he'd seen with Jenna and Rusty.

Deion looked around the circle of campers and cowboys. "You all really believe in this ghost?" he asked.

"I don't," Gordo said loudly.

Everyone looked at him. They were all about to say that they did, given what they'd seen so far.

"I don't think it's real," Gordo repeated. "And I think tomorrow we should go out and track it down."

"Gordo — is that you?" Rusty reached over to feel his friend's forehead. Teasingly, he said, "Do you have a fever?"

"You're the last one I'd think would want to go ghost hunting, Gordo," Jenna said. "Didn't Rusty practically have to drag you out here? You're not the adventurous type."

"Well, I am now," Gordo said. "And I think I know where to start looking."

He pointed ahead of the trail they had taken into camp. The shape of the cliff was like a black hole in the starry sky. "Right there," he said.

As if in answer to Gordo's challenge, a booming noise came from the direction of the cliff.

It echoed around them and spooked the horses, who tried to pull away from their posts. They looked in fright at the cliff. The sound was deafening. But what it said was familiar:

"GO AWAY, GO AWAY, GO AWAY!"

21

"Okay," said Deion as the voice faded in the night. "I guess I believe you. But Gordo's right. There's no reason to think a ghost made that noise."

"Then who was it who flew over our heads earlier?" Rusty asked.

"Maybe it was just my helicopter," Deion said, laughing.

"Well, your helicopter isn't see-through and it doesn't have a skull for a head," Jenna said.

"Good point," Deion said.

"Tomorrow, we should go find him," Gordo repeated.

"Find who?" Deion said. "The ghost?"

"That's right," Gordo said.

"Little man," Deion said, "I like your style!"

"Okay, Gordo," Emmitt said. "What's the play?"

"I think we should split up into different teams

to see what we can find," Gordo said. "That way we can cover more areas."

"Sounds good," Rusty said. "But what are we looking for? I hope you don't expect us to lasso a ghost!"

"Maybe not lasso the ghost," Gordo answered. "But maybe we can find some evidence to show where he goes." He looked at Rusty. "Some evidence that won't turn to dust when you crush it in your hand."

Rusty grimaced. "Hey, I was excited," he said. "Maybe I squeezed that old coin too hard. How was I to know it was so fragile?"

"What do you think the teams should be, Gordo?" Troy asked.

"I'd like to go with you, Troy," Jenna spoke up.

"And I'd like you as my teammate," Emmitt said quickly to Gordo.

"Then I guess that leaves you and me, Rusty," Deion said. Rusty smiled. Finally, he thought, *I've got my own Dallas Cowboy teammate!*

Shorty chipped in, too. "Well, if you all can go find this ghost and convince him to leave, go right ahead. Fats, Romario, Junior, and I can keep the cows moving until you can join up again."

"Where will we look for the ghost, Gordo?" Emmitt asked.

"I think each team should go to a different part of the cliff and the cave," Rusty said.

"Um, right, Rusty, that's what I was going to say."

"Cool," said Gordo. "How about if you and Deion ride the trail along the back of the cliff to the top. It looks pretty flat up there. You should be able to get a good view of things."

"You got it, Gordo!" Deion said. He gave Rusty a high five, a low five, an in-between five, and a four-part handshake.

"You know what that area up there is called, don't you?" Fats said as he finished cleaning up the hot chocolate mess. "That there's a *mesa*. It means 'table' in Spanish. The top of that cliff is flat and level as a table."

Gordo went on. "Then Deion and Rusty can 'set the *mesa*' for the ghost! Jenna and Troy, do you feel like checking out the cave?"

Jenna looked at Troy. He smiled and nodded back at her. "No problem, Gordo," she said. "We've just got to find a couple flashlights."

"Check," Shorty said. "I've got a couple in my saddlebag."

"Okay, Gordo," Emmitt said. "That just leaves you and me."

"I thought we should ride along the base of the cliff, or the *mesa*, I should say," Gordo replied. "By circling the entire *mesa*, we can find out where the ghost might have gone."

The three teams were silent for a minute thinking about their jobs. They were all thinking the same thing. What if there really was a ghost out there waiting to get them? Would they be too scared to do anything? Or would they be brave and face up to it?

Jenna broke the silence. "That about covers it, Gordo," she said. "We'll find this ghost by looking inside, outside, and around this cliff."

"Man, I'm so excited. I feel like the night before a big game," Emmitt said.

"Tomorrow is just like a big game, Emmitt," Gordo said. "Tomorrow, we have a ghost hunt!"

22

In the morning, the camp awakened to the smell of bacon and eggs frying. Shorty was doing his best impression of Cookie fixing up a big breakfast.

"I bet ghost hunters need a lot of energy," he said as he dished up the food.

No one answered.

After they had finished, they cleaned up the campsite. They made sure the fire was completely out (on purpose this time!) and gathered up all their gear. Bedrolls were packed into saddlebags, and canteens were filled from the water jugs. They each wrapped up some bread and cheese for a quick lunch later.

Then the three teams met to go over their plan. They huddled around Gordo, because this was all his idea.

"It's nine o'clock now," Gordo said. "Let's plan to meet by three o'clock at the cave entrance to see what's up. We can compare notes and decide what to do next."

"Have you ever thought of becoming a coach, Gordo?" Troy asked with a laugh. "You're pretty good at getting things organized."

"If I could coach players like you, I'd do it in a minute!" Gordo answered with a smile.

While Troy, Deion, and Emmitt went over to help Shorty get the cows organized for the morning drive, the three campers talked about the day ahead.

"I don't care if we find a ghost or not today," Rusty said. "I am so psyched that I'm going to spend the day with Deion Sanders!"

"Think of all the football tips I can get from Troy Aikman while exploring a cave!" Jenna said.

"I think I'm just going to enjoy being around Emmitt," Gordo said. "He's as great a guy as he is a running back."

The players returned and rejoined their teammates for the day. The three teams were ready to go.

"Wait!" Gordo said. He rode back to where Shorty was waiting to drive the herd. "Shorty," he said, "can you watch something for me?"

"Sure, pal, what is it?" Shorty asked.

Gordo reached into his saddlebag and brought out the sleeping kitten. He handed it to the camp owner. "A ghost hunt is no place for a little guy," Gordo said firmly. "We'll be back."

Then he wheeled and rode off toward the mystery *mesa* with his teammates. They would soon find out if it contained a ghost . . . or a danger even greater than that.

They rode on through the desert. The *mesa* ahead loomed larger and larger. Finally, they were only a few hundred yards away. The trail they were on forked into three parts. Deion and Rusty headed to the right to reach the path to the top of the *mesa*. Emmitt and Gordo went straight to the base of the *mesa* to explore. And Jenna and Troy turned to the left, toward the cave that was the legendary home of the Lost Cowboy Ghost.

After riding for about an hour, Jenna and Troy reached the mouth of the cave. It looked like a big black spot on the red clay walls of the *mesa*. Like Rusty had the day before, they could hear the wind whistling softly across the mouth of the cave. But without their flashlights, they couldn't see two feet inside.

"It looks spooky in there," Jenna said. "You sure you want to do this?"

"You heard the coach," Troy said with a laugh. "I always do what the coach says."

He and Jenna found rocks to tie their horses

to. Nearby, they also found the spot where Rusty had found the coin. "Look," Jenna said. "There are his footprints and Dynamite's, too."

"I guess this is the place, then," Troy said.

They tested their flashlights, grabbed their canteens, and headed in.

"Wait!" Jenna shouted. "I forgot something." She ran out of the cave and went to her horse. She pulled one other thing out of her saddlebag and ran back to Troy.

"What's that?" Troy asked.

"It's a big piece of charcoal from the campfire," Jenna answered, holding up a lump of black stuff. "Didn't you ever read about Hansel and Gretel?"

Then Troy knew what she was doing.

As they went into the cave, Jenna made a big X on the wall with the charcoal. The dark soot from the charcoal stood out against the light brown walls of the cave when they hit it with their flashlights. "I'll make a mark every once in a while," Jenna said. "That way we'll be able to find our way out."

"Good planning," Troy said. "That's the move of a smart quarterback. Lead on!"

Their flashlight beams shot into the darkness. They saw a tunnel stretching in front of them. Watching the floor carefully for rocks or hidden shafts, they proceeded into the cave.

About two hundred yards into the tunnel, Troy's flashlight lit up a series of what looked like pictures carved into the wall.

"Looks like we weren't the first ones in here," Jenna said. "Do you think the Lost Cowboy Ghost made those?"

"I don't think so," Troy said. "Those look like Native American drawings. Remember, people lived here for hundreds of years before cowboys came across the Texas plains."

They looked at the stick-figure drawings of men and animals, of the sun and the moon. Jenna thought it was eerie knowing that someone had stood on that spot so many years before. It was like looking at another kind of ghost.

After a few minutes of walking, and after making several more marks on the wall, they found that the tunnel split into two directions.

"Here's the tricky part, I guess," Troy said. "Which way should we go?"

As if in answer to his question, a voice boomed behind them.

"GO AWAY!"

Suddenly a loud rumbling sound filled the cave. Dust began to swirl around and they heard what sounded like a roaring waterfall behind them. It continued for a few minutes. Then there was total silence.

Troy and Jenna spun away from the fork and

ran back toward the entrance to see what had caused the noise — and to see if they could find the owner of that booming voice.

What they saw when they got to the cave entrance chilled their blood.

A landslide of rocks and dirt had completely covered the entrance.

They were trapped!

23

Deion and Rusty were slowly making their way up a trail on the outside of the *mesa*.

Their horses picked their hooves among the rocks on the trail. It wound back and forth up the side of the *mesa*. Rusty tried not to look down. One slip by his trusty horse Dynamite and they'd both end up falling. And it was a long way down.

Rusty looked behind him to see if Deion was keeping up. Prime Time had borrowed one of the spare horses that Shorty had brought along in case one of the campers' horses got sick or tired. Deion was riding a backup horse named Goldie.

"Goldie, huh?" Rusty had said when Deion met the horse. "Kind of like that jewelry you've got on, Prime Time."

"I just hope I'm not too heavy for this little horse," Deion had replied. "I may have to leave the jewelry behind." They laughed and Deion let Rusty try on one of the giant gold chains he was wearing, the one with the diamond #21.

But now, hundreds of feet up the side of the cliff, they weren't joking around. Riding this trail was serious business. The horses were walking along a ledge that was only about eight feet wide. They couldn't ride next to each other. Single file was the only way to make it up.

"How ya doin' up there, Rusty?" Deion called out.

"Just great, Prime Time!" Rusty answered back.

"How much farther is it? Can you see?"

"I think I see the end of the trail up ahead," Rusty called back. After riding up the side of the *mesa*, they finally reached the top.

Both riders dismounted to give their horses a rest after the hard climb. They praised their mounts, too, and gave them a snack of carrots that Shorty had given them.

"This is harder than I thought it would be," Deion said, rubbing his back pockets. "How come these things don't come with pads?"

"I said the same thing, Deion," Rusty said. "But you'll get used to it."

"I hope we find this ghost soon," Deion said. "Otherwise, I'm going to have to have my chopper fly in a motorcycle. I don't care what that pest Aikman says." They laughed at the thought of Deion screaming around the prairie on a motorcycle.

110

Deion looked over the *mesa* top and said, "Hey, this looks like a good place for a football field! Maybe even two or three!"

"Just make sure you don't run too far out of bounds," Rusty said, pointing to the edge of the cliff. "It's a long way down!"

They took a minute to admire the view. From on top of the cliff, they could see for miles. The taller mountains in the distance rose up jagged and sharp to meet the sky. In between was the big Texas prairie. It looked like a big brown carpet stretched out on the floor. Other *mesas* and smaller hills dotted the landscape like some giant hand had just tossed them there.

"Look, you can see the herd from here," Rusty said. He pointed back toward where they had come from. The herd of cows looked like a bunch of beetles scurrying on a floor.

Looking in the other direction, they could barely make out the buildings of Shorty's ranch. A small wisp of smoke rose from one of the buildings. "That must be the cook tent," Rusty said.

After their rest break, they got back on their mounts and began looking for signs of the ghost or anything else they could find. The sand didn't show any footprints or hoofprints other than their own. But Rusty found one unusual thing.

"Hey, Deion," he called. "Look at this!"

"What did you find, Rusty?"

Rusty pointed to an area of sandy soil that was

completely unmarked. No rocks, no tracks, nothing. It looked as if it had been flattened by a large weight.

"That looks like a big rectangle," Rusty said. "You can see where it stops here." He pointed to a sharp line in the sand. On one side, the sand was bare and flat. On the other it was filled with rocks, sticks, and weeds.

"If it was smaller, I'd say Nate Newton had sat here," Deion laughed, thinking of his oversized Dallas teammate.

"But this area is so big, it looks like the whole offensive line stomped on it for a week!" Rusty said.

He walked carefully across the edge of the big rectangle. It was seven long paces across and five paces wide. Then he put his foot gingerly on the stomped sand. Nothing happened, so he walked to the center of the square. He looked out on the prairie from where he stood.

"I wonder what this was," Rusty said.

"I don't know," Deion said. "Maybe the ghost's launching pad."

They continued on and, as they rode, they saw another of the flat-sand squares. Toward the far edge of the *mesa* from where they had started, they found a third one. But this third square was a bit smaller than the other two. And long, thin trails in the sand led away from the square.

"Those look too small to have been made by

snakes," Deion said, scratching his head. "They almost look like wires."

Rusty walked onto the square as he had done with the first one. "I can see the cook tent even better from here," he said.

And then the ground started moving under his feet. It shook back and forth and he was jolted off his feet. The sand on the square began spinning like a whirlpool.

Suddenly a crack in the square opened! The sand started slipping into it. And Rusty was falling in, too!

"Deion!" he yelled. "Help! I'm being sucked in!" He scrambled, trying to grab something to keep from being pulled in. Deion reached for Rusty's hand, but they were too far apart.

The ground continued to tilt downward and Rusty slid slowly, slowly into the hole. Finally, just his head and arms were visible.

Then Rusty vanished, falling into the earth!

Without waiting a second, Deion dived in after him.

Then the ground shook again, the crack in the earth closed, and the two teammates were gone!

24

Gordo and Emmitt slowly walked their horses along the base of the cliff.

"What exactly are we looking for, Gordo?" Emmitt asked when they stopped for a moment to rest.

"I don't know," Gordo said. "But all these things that have happened to us have centered around this *mesa*."

"Except for the warning on the bus!" Emmitt pointed out.

"Right," Gordo said. He got a thoughtful look. "That's true. That was the only time the ghost actually did anything in the camp itself. Otherwise, it did all its haunting out here."

"And remember," Emmitt added, "no one ever saw the ghost in the camp except those cowboys who ran away. The only time we've seen it is when it flew off the cliff and over our heads."

Flying ghosts, scary messages, mysterious voices in the desert. *If this keeps up*, Gordo thought, *no one will ever want to come out here. Shorty's camp will turn into a ghost town! A real ghost town with a real ghost!*

But Gordo still wasn't convinced. "Let's keep looking, Emmitt," he said firmly. "There's more to this than meets the eye."

Emmitt smiled with pride at his friend's determination. "Gordo," he said, "when I get to the Super Bowl again, you're coming with me to cheer me on. I like your spirit!"

Gordo was beaming when he climbed back onto Brains. Emmitt hopped up on Touchdown and they continued their search.

As they went around a big rock at the base of the cliff, Emmitt brought his horse to a stop. "Gordo!" he called. "Look at this!"

The two friends looked down at a series of footprints that sunk deep into the dirt. They were coated with a fine white dust.

Gordo leaped off his horse to examine them.

"Did the ghost make them?" Emmitt said.

Gordo carefully felt the footprints. He followed them with his eyes as they wandered along the prairie floor. Then he looked more closely at the footprints.

"No," he said finally. "No ghost made these footprints."

"Then what's that white stuff?" Emmitt asked. "And how come you're so sure?"

"Simple," Gordo said. "These prints were made

a long time ago. Look how hard the dirt is around them. They were made when the dirt was soft, like after a rain. And it hasn't rained here for quite a while. Also, the ghost we saw wore cowboy boots. Whoever made these prints wore sandals or moccasins. See, no heel marks!"

Emmitt was impressed with Gordo's detective work.

"But what about that white powder?"

Gordo pointed to a rock sticking out from the cliff face. "Chalk," he said simply. "It looks like a bird used this as a perch. And it must have pecked off some of the chalk, which fell on the footprints. See, here are some claw marks."

"Gordo, you're a regular Sherlock Holmes!" Emmitt said.

"That must make you Doctor Watson!" Gordo said. He jumped back onto Brains and they continued their search.

A short while later, Gordo noticed an unusual mark in the sand. "What do you think those lines are, Emmitt?" He pointed to a series of long, thin trails in the sand, trails just like the ones Rusty and Deion had found on top of the *mesa*.

"I'm not sure, Gordo," Emmitt said. "Snake tracks?"

"Too thin to be snakes," Gordo said.

Then Emmitt remembered where he'd seen similar tracks. It was in Green Bay a few seasons before. "Hey, Gordo," he said. "We played the Packers on a cold, snowy day last year. The field was cleared, but the show stayed thick on the sidelines. When the coaches walked back and forth wearing their headsets, they left long, thin trails in the snow.

"Gordo!" Emmitt said. "Could these tracks be wires too?"

"Good call, Emmitt," Gordo said. "But what would wires be doing out here?"

As soon as he said that, they heard a loud scraping sound up ahead. They looked up suddenly. About 200 yards ahead of them, the rock face was opening up! A huge boulder was rolling to one side, revealing a door into the *mesa*!

As they watched in amazement, a ghostly white figure of a man on horseback rode around the edge of the cliff and into the door. And then it shut behind him. The rock face looked just as it had before. The figure had disappeared.

At first, Gordo felt scared in spite of himself. Then he had a thought.

"Since when do ghosts need doors?" Gordo said, no longer afraid.

"Let's go!" Emmitt yelled.

The two detectives galloped toward the home of the Lost Cowboy Ghost!

25

Troy and Jenna stared at the pile of rocks that blocked the entrance to the cave. No light showed through the mass of stone and earth. Some of the boulders were as tall as Troy. There was no way they could dig their way out.

The air was moist and sticky in the cave. The gloom around them seemed deeper without any sunlight. And now there was no wind whispering softly across the cave mouth. The cave felt like a big box with the lid tightly closed.

Jenna was shaking her head. "No, no, this can't be happening!" she said. "We can't be stuck here! This is terrible."

"It's okay, Jenna," Troy said. "As long as we stick together, we can find a way out of this."

Jenna took a deep breath and let it out. She was glad Troy was with her. "You're right, Troy. Panic won't get us out of here."

"That's the way to think," Troy said. "Here's what we should do. Pretend you're quarterbacking a team one day, and all your passes to one side of the field aren't working. What would you do?"

Halfheartedly, Jenna answered, "That's easy, go the other direction. Pass to the other side of the field." She paused. "Hey! I get it! We'll go the other direction!"

"There's always another way to do things," Troy said. "If we can't get out this way, we'll just keep on going *into* the cave until we find a way out."

"Right!" Jenna said. "We'll just keep going!"

Neither one of them said what they were thinking: That if there wasn't another way out of this game, this is one trip that wouldn't have a happy ending.

They made their way back into the cave, passing the cave drawings and Jenna's X marks again. They came to the fork.

"Right or left?" Troy asked.

"I don't know," Jenna said. "How about we flip for it?"

"Like before a football game," Troy said. "I've got a coin here. Heads we go right, tails we go left. Okay?"

"Okay," Jenna said.

He flipped the coin and they watched it turn over and over.

The coin landed with a soft plop in the dust on the cave floor. They searched with their flashlights until they saw something sparkle. "Heads!" Troy said and picked up the coin.

"Hey, wait a minute!" he said. "This isn't the coin I flipped! I flipped a quarter and this is an old silver dollar." He handed it to Jenna.

She examined it with the flashlight. "Look, it says 1875, just like the one Rusty said he found!" Jenna said.

Troy picked up another coin. "Now here is the one I flipped," he said. "Guess what? It was heads, too!"

Jenna put the silver dollar carefully in her pocket. "I guess that settles it. To the right we go!"

They kept walking. Jenna kept making marks on the wall in case they had to find the fork in the tunnel trail again.

As they walked along, Jenna noticed that the walls were getting smoother and smoother. And the dust on the floor was getting thinner and thinner.

"This doesn't look like any cave I've seen pictures of," she said finally. "It looks more like cardboard than rock!"

Troy felt the wall. "You're right," he said. "It feels like someone has carved these tunnels. They don't feel rough or uneven at all. Someone has definitely been down here."

"Sure," Jenna said. "The Native American drawings told us that."

"Yes," Troy answered, "but those were near the natural entrance to the cave. This tunnel looks much newer than the entrance."

Suddenly, they heard a soft sound like two pillows being smashed together. Then they heard faint sounds coming from the tunnel ahead.

"Sounds like we're not alone, Jenna," Troy said.

"Well, I'm certainly not running away," she said. "There's no way out back the way we came."

They advanced slowly, their flashlights showing the way.

The tunnel floor slowly sloped upward. At the end of the tunnel was a dark archway. The sounds were getting louder.

"I guess this is it," Troy whispered.

"Looks like we've found something," Jenna said. "I hope it's just a way out and not a way to the ghost."

"Let's go for it!" Troy whispered urgently.

They charged into the archway, flashlights shining ahead of them.

And they stopped short!

The bright beams of the flashlights lit up a pair of figures.

Two ghosts! thought Jenna. *This is too much!*

26

After the earth closed above Rusty and Deion's heads, they fell into the wildest ride of their lives. Sputtering sand out of their mouths, they were sliding downhill fast, out of control!

They were in a long, twisting tube like at a water slide, but there was no water. They slid around and around, tumbling and turning. The tube was pitch-black and they never knew where the next twist would take them.

They were moving too fast to speak. Each bang and bump around the tube echoed, drowning out any conversation.

As Rusty swooped around another 360-degree circle, all the while continuing down, down into the *mesa*, he was thinking, *I hope there's a soft landing wherever this thing is taking us!*

He could hear Deion sliding behind him, sometimes next to him, in the big tunnel. Finally, they stopped spinning and were sliding down a long, straight section that was not as steep as before. Then they were slowing down.

Rusty could see a dim light at the end of the tunnel. *This is it*, he thought. *We're there! We made it!*

They shot out through the end of the tunnel and PLOOSH! landed next to each other on a huge pile of foam rubber pads. *It's like falling into a bag of marshmallows*, thought Rusty.

"Wow! What a ride!" Deion yelled. "Hey, Rusty! Are you okay?"

Rusty lay there in the pads for a moment, catching his breath. He waited until his body stopped spinning. *Nope, nothing hurt*, he thought. Now that he knew the ending was a happy one on this ride, he wanted to go back up to do it again!

"I'm fine, Deion," Rusty said. "I'm a little dizzy, but that was sort of fun! Thank goodness for these pads!"

"Yeah," Deion said. "Otherwise we'd be a couple of flat cowboys."

"Hey Deion, thanks for coming in after me," Rusty said. "Sorry I got you into this."

"It wasn't your fault there was some kind of trapdoor up there, Rusty," Deion said. "Besides, I wouldn't rather be anywhere else. Where my teammates go, I go!"

They slowly climbed out of the pit of pads and hopped down from the platform where they had landed.

"Speaking of which," Deion said, "where are we?"

The pair looked around the giant room where they had landed. It was bigger than a classroom back in Dallas, with tall walls that reached into the darkness above. In one wall of the room, they could see the slide tube exit from which they had come. There was an archway in the opposite wall, but it was pitch-black beyond the arch.

The walls looked like they had been carved out of the rock itself. The floor was covered with a fine dust, but it looked clean and neat . . . for a cave, that is.

Next to another wall stood a huge black box. From the back of it came a series of wires. "Hey, look, Deion," Rusty said, pointing to the wires. "You might have been right about those wires."

He walked carefully around the box, counting his steps and measuring it. "It's as big as those flat squares we found on the *mesa*," he said. "They must have been up there at one time and flattened out the sand."

"Yeah," Deion said. "But what are they? There are no marks anywhere. It looks like a big black refrigerator, but there's no door!"

They found another, smaller black box in the corner of the room, along with some small square packages that looked like computer disks.

Rusty was about to look at them more closely when they heard noises coming from the arch. He dropped the disks and ran back to where Deion was looking at the black box.

The sounds were getting closer and closer! Footsteps were getting louder and louder! Deion and Rusty looked frantically for a place to hide.

Just then, something raced into the room. Rusty and Deion looked at the arch.

Suddenly, two bright beams of light shot out of the arch.

They were trapped like deer in headlights! There was nowhere to hide!

We may have landed safely after our wild ride, Rusty thought, while he shielded his eyes from the light, *but we're in big trouble now!*

27

After watching the ghostly rider go into the rocky doorway, Gordo and Emmitt had raced ahead to try to follow it. But the door was closed shut when they got there.

"Look, you can see the edge of the door here," Gordo said. They had climbed down off their horses and were examining the rock face the ghost had ridden through.

"Here's another edge," Emmitt said. The door they had discovered was about five yards across. Hoofprints led up to it, then disappeared into the rock.

Ghost horses don't make hoofprints, thought Gordo. If they hadn't seen the door open, they would have been baffled. But now they knew the secret. Unless the Lost Cowboy Ghost was the first ghost ever to need a door!

"How do you think it opens?" Emmitt asked. "There's no handle, no knob, not even a keyhole."

They carefully checked out every inch of the

rock but found nothing that told them how to open the door.

"Maybe it's like an electric garage door," Gordo said. "We use a remote control to open our garage."

"Well, we don't have the remote, unfortunately," Emmitt sighed. "Maybe there's another switch outside somewhere. Most garage doors have that, too."

But another examination of the rock surrounding the door led nowhere.

They were stumped. They had come so far and were so close to solving the mystery of the Lost Cowboy Ghost. But now they could go no further.

Gordo hoped his friends were doing better than he was. And he hoped they were okay.

"We've just got to get in there," Gordo said. "But how?"

Behind them, the two horses were chewing contentedly on some grass near a group of rocks. Brains was tugging at one clump of weeds when he accidentally kicked over one of the rocks that was standing up like a stump.

THUMP!

Gordo and Emmitt whirled around at the sound of the rock falling over.

"It was just the horses," Emmitt said with a sigh of relief. Then he and Gordo heard a squeaking sound coming from the rock face. They turned to face it again.

The door was opening!

"Way to go!" Gordo shouted to his horse. "Brains found the key! No wonder he's named that."

The two teammates waited at the side of the doorway as it opened slowly. It revealed a long tunnel leading into the heart of the *mesa*!

Small lights shone from the ceiling of the tunnel as it made its way back into the rock.

"Should we go in?" Emmitt asked.

"Of course," Gordo said. "We're hunting a ghost. And a ghost went in here."

The pair slipped inside the doorway and began walking down the tunnel. Suddenly the door slammed shut behind them!

"I hope we can find the switch on this side without any help from Brains," Gordo said.

"I hope we have the chance to try," Emmitt said with a worried look.

They moved slowly up the tunnel. It seemed to slope upward as they walked. Their boots thumped hollowly on the hard dirt floor of the tunnel. They could see hoofprints in the dust leading in both directions . . . in and out of the *mesa*.

"This must be where the horse rode in and out," Gordo said. "Whoever was riding it."

They saw a brighter light up ahead. It was over a tall, square doorway that spanned the width of the tunnel. There was a button on one side.

"Should we push it?" Emmitt asked.

"Let's see if we can hear what's on the other side first," Gordo suggested.

They put their ears to the wooden door.

When they heard what was on the other side, they both made a mad dash to push the button!

"We've got to get in there fast!" Gordo said.

"Or our teammates are done for!" Emmitt said.

Gordo stabbed the button with his thumb. And on soft, silent hinges, the giant door swung open!

28

The light burst into Deion's and Rusty's eyes. Troy and Jenna stared at the two figures in the beam of their flashlights.

And then all four of them began high-fiving.

"We thought you were the ghost!" Rusty said.

"We thought you guys were!" Jenna shouted.

The tube from the top of the *mesa* and the tunnel from the cave entrance both had ended in the big room with the black boxes.

Rusty quickly told Troy and Jenna how they had ended up in the room.

"That sounds like a wild ride, Rusty," Jenna said. "Too bad it's not at an amusement park."

Then Rusty noticed how dusty and dirty Troy and Jenna were. "What happened to you guys?"

"Someone started a cave-in at the entrance to the cave," Troy said. "Looks like the only way out now is that tube you all slid through."

"That tube was as slippery as oil," Deion said.

"I don't know how we can climb out of it."

Jenna noticed the big box. "What's that?" she said.

"We were just trying to figure that out," Rusty said, "when you ghost chasers found us."

The group examined the box again. This time, Rusty also noticed that there was sand caked on the bottom edges of the box. At one time, they must have been on the *mesa* top!

"There's a switch on the back," Troy said. He flicked it.

The voice of the Lost Cowboy Ghost rang out in the small room.

"GO AWAY! GO AWAY! GO AWAY!"

Then Troy flicked the switch again and the voice stopped.

"A giant speaker! That's where the voice that we heard came from!" Rusty exclaimed. "I'm beginning to think Gordo was right."

Jenna was checking out the other box, the one with the disks. "Look at this," she said. She had taken the cover off the box and discovered what looked like a slide projector.

"What is it?" asked Deion.

"I'm not sure," Jenna said. "But here's a switch. Should I turn it on?"

"Go for it!" Rusty said.

Jenna flicked the switch.

Suddenly, the Lost Cowboy Ghost appeared in

the air over their heads! He galloped around the room, flying through the air just as he had on the prairie the day before!

Jenna quickly flicked the switch again. The ghostly vision vanished.

"It's a hologram!" Jenna shouted. "A hologram of a ghost on a horse!"

"Well," Rusty said, "it looks like we've found the Lost Cowboy Ghost!"

Just then a deep, growling voice echoed through the room.

"You sure have!" the voice said.

They all whirled around to see where it was coming from.

From the far corner of the room, a tall figure surrounded in ghostly white light advanced on them. As he got closer, they could all see that beneath a glowing white cowboy hat was nothing but a skull!

And it wasn't smiling!

The deep, growling voice came directly from the skull this time, not from the big black speaker box.

"And now you Cowboys have played your last game!"

29

The Lost Cowboy Ghost stopped when he got about ten yards away from the group. Then, to their horror, he reached up and pulled off his face!

It was a mask!

Underneath the mask was not a ghost, but a man. The Lost Cowboy Ghost was the missing cowboy Rex!

"You all should listen to what people tell you!" he said angrily. "I told you to go away and you didn't listen! Now you're going to be trapped in here forever!"

Rusty looked at the bizarre figure in front of him. Rex's head was normal, but his body glowed as if it were made of light. Then Rusty remembered a science class experiment he had done. Rex had obviously covered his clothing with phosphorescent paint. It glowed in any kind of light!

"I'm going to go out that door behind me, and

seal you in here," Rex continued. "The only way out is up that tube, and there's no way you'll ever climb it. You'll soon be the Lost 'Dallas Cowboy' Ghosts!" He looked at Rusty and Jenna. "And friends!" he added with a menacing laugh.

"Why are you doing all this?" Troy asked, stalling for time.

"Shorty never treated me right," Rex said. "He was always giving me the dirty jobs to do. So when some real estate guys wanted to get him off his land to build a new desert resort, they hired me to scare him off. When he started telling that stupid old Lost Cowboy Ghost legend, I made it come to life."

He waved his hand around the room. "With the help of the real estate guys, I just added on to these old mining tunnels and made a home for the ghost." He pointed to the boxes. "I see you discovered how the ghost flew over your heads! That was great. I was watching with binoculars from the *mesa*. You should have seen your faces! Ha-ha! You all were as white as the ghost!"

Jenna wasn't scared. She was angry.

"Then it was you who ripped my autographed Emmitt Smith photo on the bus!" she shouted.

"That's right, kid," Rex answered. "I never liked them Dallas dudes anyway. I hate football."

Rex sneered. "That just adds to my pleasure of getting Shorty off his land," he said. "When people hear how dangerous his camp is, they'll stop coming. I already scared off almost all the men who work for him."

"That's where we came in, pal," Troy said. "You didn't figure on having some cowboys who wouldn't scare!"

"Yeah," Rex said. "That made it tough. But you're just like the rest of them. I'll get rid of you, too."

He began to back up toward the door behind him. The four ghost chasers didn't know what to do next. Should they rush him? Should they try to get past him? He was only one person and they were four. They'd have a good chance.

But they waited too long. The door swung open behind him. He was only a few steps from freedom. And they were only a few seconds from being buried forever in the mystery *mesa*.

Would this be the final play for Troy Aikman and Deion Sanders?

30

Suddenly, Emmitt and Gordo busted into the room!

Emmitt drove his shoulder into Rex and tackled him to the ground. Troy and Deion leaped to help their teammate tackle the rotten cowboy! He struggled, but it was no good. The Cowboys had won again!

Jenna and Rusty rushed over to see Gordo!

"Way to go, Gordo!" Jenna yelled and hugged him.

"Just in the nick of time, dude!" Rusty shouted. "You were awesome! But where did you come from?"

"We were listening to Rex from the other side of the door," Gordo said. He pointed to the door that led to the tunnel they had found. "We heard everything you and he said. When he said he was leaving, we knew we had to get in here to help out!"

"Well, you were sure in the right place at the

right time!" Rusty said. "I thought we were going to have to dig our way out of this *mesa!*"

The three friends looked over to where the three Dallas Cowboys were tying up Rex.

"Hey, Rex," Deion laughed. "If you promise to be nice, I'll send you an autographed picture to hang in your cell!" He aimed a full-on Neon Deion smile at the angry fake ghost.

"Forget you, Sanders," he snarled. "I'd rather look at a blank wall than a picture of you."

"You guys did a great job," Emmitt said. "You worked together and you tracked down the ghost. You should be very proud of yourselves."

"You should be pretty proud yourself, Emmitt," Troy said. "That was a great tackle you made."

"Well, even us offensive players have to be defensive sometimes, right Deion?" Emmitt said with a laugh.

"Emmitt," Deion said, "sometimes we can even be both!"

31

The next day everyone was back at the Six Points Ranch just in front of the storm. The police had taken Rex away. The cattle had been corralled by Shorty, Fats, and the others. Now it was time for the campers to continue their week of fun in the Western sun . . . once the rain dried, that is.

First, though, there were some good-byes to say.

With their work done, and the camp once again safe from ghosts and creepy real estate goons, the Dallas Cowboys had to get back to Dallas to get ready for their NFL training camp.

"We're really sorry we have to leave," Emmitt said. "But Shorty can tell you, there's nothing a coach hates worse than players who show up late."

"You sure never tried that one on me," Shorty said with a laugh. "Or you would have been running laps until your shoes fell off! Really, though, thanks for everything, you guys, we couldn't have done it without you."

Gordo and Jenna shook hands with Troy, Emmitt, and Deion.

"We'll be cheering for you this season," Jenna said. "Bring us back another Super Bowl title!"

"We'll do our best," Troy said. "You can count on that."

"Definitely," Deion said. "You can count on Prime Time!"

"Hey, where's Rusty?" Emmitt asked. "We want to say good-bye to him, but we've really got to get going."

Just then a booming voice rang out over the desert. *Not again*, thought Jenna.

"PLEASE STAY! PLEASE STAY!" the voice said.

Rusty stepped out from behind the bunkhouse, holding a microphone.

"Rusty must have found Rex's speakers after we brought them back to camp this morning," Gordo said.

Rusty waved and spoke into the microphone again. His voice boomed over the ranch.

"DALLAS COWBOYS RULE!"

Everyone cheered as the three NFL stars rode off into the sunset.

In Deion's helicopter.